PAINT CONTRACTORS BUSINESS MANUAL

By Kevin McGeer

To receive your CD-ROM templates, log onto www.franchisekit.co.za and follow instructions

Publisher: Franchise Kit
Cover design: Clive Thompson www.getclive.com
Production and composition: Franchise Kit, Po Box 1559 Hillcrest 3650 South Africa and www.createspace.com.

First edition: Paint Contracting Business Manual

This publication is designed to provide authoritive information in regard to the subject matter covered. It is sold with the understanding that the publisher is not rendering legal, accounting or other professional services. If legal advice or other expert assistance is required, the services of a competent professional person should be sought.

ISBN: 978-0-620-50876-6
*CD-ROM unique number: **67823***
Printed in South Africa by Pinetown Printers and by Create Space in USA

Disclaimer:
 While every care has been taken in completing this document, no representation, warranty, guarantee or undertaking (express or implied) is given and no responsibility nor liability is accepted by Franchise Kit nor its directors, employees or agents either as to the accuracy of the information provided or for any consequence that may result from any assignment. Franchise Kit's liability shall in no case exceed its invoice price and it shall not be liable for any consequential loss.

Meet the author

Kevin McGeer has worked in the paint contracting field in England, America, Australia and South Africa. He has learnt the tricks of the trade over 25 years, having built up the largest paint contacting company in South Africa with over 40 branches. He has learnt the hard way through tried and tested practical applications, leaving him with cutting edge experience.

He has also painted in all the markets including industrial, commercial, domestic and new construction. He also has vast experience in coating specifications, general painting, water-proofing, surface preparation and damp-proofing. His professional approach has made him master of this profitable trade.

His formal business qualifications combined with his paint contracting knowledge and experience make him one of the world's leading authorities in this exciting field.

Acknowledgements

There are so many people who have had influences in my life that have made this book possible. My family Maryke and Stuart have stood by me in all the years of the ups and downs of just being in business – but I am sure that they will agree that paint contracting has given us far more ups than downs.

My father taught me the realities of business, the fast and hard way. We were business partners in paint contracting for over a decade and had fun with a full learning curve back in the 1980's

The suppliers in our industry have been supportive pillars. They have educated me and have been patient in all my undertakings in the paint industry.

The numerous friends, who have been sounding boards and who have assisted with writing improved and new business plans on the back of till slips.

But the most important people to thank are the actual painters, for without them this dream would not be true. They are the eyes and mouth-pieces for us in our businesses.

I thank all the individuals who have had influences in my life and who have made the dream of this book come true. And I wish all those who take the time to read it, good luck in this exciting and profitable business environment.

Kevin McGeer

CONTENTS

PART 1 – INTRODUCTION   12
1. Introduction to the book and templates
2. Why paint contracting?
3. Why paint contracting businesses fail?
4. Market trends
5. What services can you offer?
6. Notes on Waterproofing, Damp-proofing and Protective Coatings
7. Mission and vision statement
8. Strategy - MOST
9. Seasons and the weather

PART 2 – STARTING YOUR BUSINESS   23
1. How simple can it be?
2. "Sale to invoice" plan – the lifecycle of paint contractors
3. Setting up your home office
4. Your business at a glance
5. Equipment to start your business

PART 3 – PAINT MANUFACTURERS   28
1. Working with your paint supplier
2. Specifications
3. Accounts
4. Delivery
5. Guarantees
6. Colour consistency and choice
7. Training

PART 4 – MARKETING   32
1. Segmenting the markets
2. Competitive analysis
3. Research your area
4. Website
5. Sales and marketing control
6. The 5 P's of marketing
7. Promotion explained further
8. The weekly diary
9. The quotation pipeline
10. Sales preparation
11. Boundary wall / Roof letter

12. Rate us
13. Company profile
14. Outline for a rep
15. Telephone script
16. Keeping photographic records
17. Corporate clothing
18. Signage

PART 5 – THE QUOTATION   **49**
1. Overview
2. What clients expect?
3. Quotation reference number
4. Index
5. Analysis of sub-strata
6. Assessments
7. Scope of work and specifications
8. Paint supplier recommendations and site inspections
9. Company details
10. References
11. Terms and conditions

PART 6 – SERVICE CONTRACT AND GUARANTEE   **54**
1. Service contract
2. Guarantee
3. How the paint manufacturers play their role

PART 7 – MANAGEMENT INFORMATION SYSTEMS   **56**
1. How to record and file information
2. Contract completed records

PART 8 – TRAINING   **57**
1. Training – In-house
2. Training – Paint suppliers

PART 9 – COSTING   **59**
1. How to estimate a contract
2. Symbols for costing
3. Tools for costing
4. Formulae's to assist with costing
5. Quotation check list
6. Overview of costing
7. Dry and wet film thickness

8. Material spread rate
9. Labour calculations
10. Case study
11. Reading plans / blue prints
12. Advanced average spread rate
13. Additional costing information
PART 10 – PRODUCTION   73
1. Budgeting the contract
2. Production schedule
3. Check list when starting a contract
4. Check list when completing a contract
5. Site control paperwork
6. Site preparation
7. Doing the painting
8. Quality control
9. Staff site register
10. Visitors register
11. House keeping
12. Stock control
13. Purchases
14. Notice to start painting
15. Notice when painting is completed
PART 11 – EQUIPMENT AND TOOLS   87
1. Spray guns
2. Hydro-blasters
3. Scaffolding
4. Step ladders
5. Moisture meter
6. Paint brushes and rollers
7. Stirrers and mixing paint
8. Drop sheets or drop cloths
9. Masking
10. Painters tool kit
11. Caulking gun
12. Power sanders
13. Roller poles and extensions
14. Power roller

15. Paint scrapers
PART 12 – SAFETY   **98**
1. Hard hats
2. Safety harnesses
3. Safety shoes
4. Gloves
5. Goggles and eye protection
6. Ladders
7. Scaffolding
8. Masks for inhalation and respirators
PART 13 – DEALING WITH LABOUR   **101**
1. Sub-contractors vs. hiring your own labour
2. Finding and keeping the right people
3. Rewards and incentives
4. Contracts
5. Sub contractors fees
PART 14 – FINANCE   **104**
1. Financial accounting vs. financial management
2. Cash flow
3. Projections
4. Example of a balance sheet
5. Invoice samples
6. Finance
7. Factoring
8. Invoice file
9. Banks file
10. Management accounts on a monthly basis
11. Keep debtors days to 7
12. Pay 90% of creditors on a cash basis
13. Petty cash
14. Break even analysis
PART 15 – CORPORATE GOVERNANCE   **118**
1. Legal entities
2. Bank accounts
3. Tax
4. Municipal bye laws
PART 16 – PLANNING FOR GROWTH   **118**

1. Expansion is limited to resources
2. Increasing profits not volumes
3. Learn to say no – Don't overtrade

PART 17 – PAINT CONTRACTING SECRETS   **120**
1. Cherry pickers
2. Subcontract labour
3. Damp vs. waterproofing
4. Masking equipment
5. Spray painting
6. **PART 18 – A FINAL WORD**   **122**

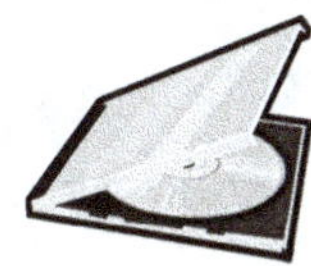

PART 19 – TEMPLATES AND BLANK FORMS ON DISK

	Pages
A. Business plan	
A1 – MOST	2
A2 - Business plan template	20
A3 - Check list when starting your business	2
A4 - Equipment check list to start your business	1
B. Production forms	
B1- File cover	1
B2 - Actual costing	1
B3 - Budget costing	1
B4 – Production schedule	1
B5 - Quality plan	1
B6 - Check list when starting a contract	1
B7 - Check list when finishing a contract	1
B8 - Staff site register	1
B9 – Visitors register	1
B10 –Notice to start painting	1
B11 – Notice to finish painting	1
B12 – Subcontractors fees	1
B13 - Final release certificate	1
B14 - Inspection & test report	1

B15 - Psychometric data: Relative Humidity   1
B16 - Psychometric data: Steel Temp   1

C. Marketing
C1 - Company profile   4
C2 - Boundary wall / Roof letter   1
C3 - How do you rate our service?   1
C4 - Advertising schedule   1
C5 – Research Questionnaire   1

D. Quotation
D1 - Quotation sample   9
D2 - Quotation check list   2
D3 - Guarantee sample   2
D4 - Service contract sample   2
D5 – Specifications   1

E. Finance
E1 - Cash flow projections   2
E2 - Invoice template   1

F. Human resource management
F1 - Contract of employment   4

G. **Safety**   60
1. Corporate health & safety policy statement
2. Health & safety specification
   2.1 Purpose
   2.2 Applicability
   2.3 Normative references
   2.4 Definitions
   2.5 Responsibilities
   2.6 Task & hazard identification
   2.7 Additional requirements
3. Site establishment check list for contractors
4. Appointment of the assistant construction supervisor
5. Appointment of the batch plant supervisor
6. Appointment of the site health & safety officer
7. Appointment of the construction supervisor
8. Appointment of the fall protection plan developer
9. Appointment of the fire extinguisher inspector
10. Appointment of the formwork and support work supervisor

11. Appointment of the ladder supervisor
12. Appointment of the material hoist inspector
13. Appointment of the construction site risk assessor
14. Appointment of the scaffolding risk assessor
15. Appointment of the suspended platform supervisor
16. Scaffolding assessment list
17. Competent person scaffold inspection check list
18. First aid box equipment check list
19. Hand tools and equipment check list
20. Hazardous substance check list
21. Walking-walking surfaces
22. Ladder inspection check list
23. Personal protection check list
24. Portable electrical tools register
25. Public safety check list
26. Roofing check list
27. Appointment first aid officer
28. Equipment register
29. Stepladder inspection form
30. Scaffolding inspection form
31. Incident report form
32. Safety work procedures – ladders
33. Safety work procedures – heights
34. Heath & safety responsibilities
35. Health & safety representative
36. Joint health & safety representative
37. Safety support staff
38. Workers
39. Subcontractors
40. Safety training
41. General safety & equipment

H. Paint problems
H1 - Paint problems – interior   23
H2 - Paint problems – exterior   25
I. Glossary   13

PART 1 – INTRODUCTION 

1. Introduction to the manual and templates on CD-ROM

This comprehensive Paint Contractors Business Manual is to assist:
*   Someone thinking of getting into paint contracting and
*   The existing paint contractor who wants to expand and run his business more profitably.
*   It is not only the paint contractor, but waterproofing, damp-proofing and protective coatings contractors.

This book does not intend to explain the different specifications of painting systems used in the many types of protective paint contracting, but rather attempts to guide the owner of the paint contracting business through the minefields and opportunities that the owner will experience.

In our competitive environment, we need all the tools to help us succeed. I have been in the paint contracting field for over twenty years and have helped build up an existing paint contracting company from humble beginnings to a company employing over 400 employees, then later I started and built up my own paint contracting company and then expanded that company nationally through franchising.

You need an edge at every corner, in order to be better than your competitors and to make more margin than you used to.

Some people think that paint contracting companies are only run by blue collar workers, who struggle to do anything else. I have sat at dinner parties where snobs hear I am in paint contracting. They think I do eclectic or nevus painting (since they hear I have made money somehow, and forbid that it is with a pickup truck hiring blue collar laborers)

I have seen doctors, lawyers and accountants running highly successful paint contracting companies, who would not swap their new careers back to their old ones for anything. I have also seen many women running their own painting teams, having fun and making loads of money. Running a successful paint contracting company, actually can free up your time. You can actually operate your company as a project management company and outsource almost all functions.

Paint contracting, run properly, is a highly sophisticated business, with the help of all the business tools that one can get.

This manual has been written for exactly that purpose – to assist you in making better decisions and making higher margins.

Included are over 200 pages of templates, (When this icon appears, it means that there is template on the CD-ROM that relates to that specific topic) to assist you in streamlining your business. These templates are in Microsoft Word and Excel 2007. You may have to download a buffer program to read them if you do not have this program.

Pease note that this book deals mostly with the business side of running your pant contracting business and does not allow for the corporate governance, health and safety issues, special licenses needed and so on of each specific area or city you may live in. Use this book as a guideline to these issues and do your research. You can change any number with a $ sign to reflect your own currency.

So enjoy the book as a reference manual and email me with any questions you may have at info@franchisekit.co.za or visit www.franchisekit.co.za.

Kevin McGeer

2. Why paint contracting

Paint contracting has many pluses on its side.

Firstly it is an annuity business. That means two things: Firstly all building assets need continuous painting and maintenance. This may differ depending on climate, such as coastal corrosion, proximity to harsh environments such as pollution fall out from industry and the general upkeep that asset owners do to their buildings.

Secondly if you receive business from a client who is in the position to give you ongoing contracts, then this too, can be seen as annuity business.

Paint contracting is not seasonal. It is one of the few businesses that continues all year round. Some clients want to spend money before their financial year end and others before the year end. Then some want the painting done in winter so the rain does not interfere with the process, if you are living in a summer rainfall area. (The same is applicable for a winter rainfall area).

Generally contracts are given all year round.

Thirdly, it is cash-flow positive (Most of the time). Clients usually pay a deposit, so labour is taken care of. Paint is usually on a 30 day account and interim draws or part invoicing is the norm for the contracting industry.

Forth, you can split your client base into small, medium and large clients to assist with seasons and cash flow. This also assists with the type of markets you have identified and therefore receive work on an ongoing basis.

Fifth, it is a business that does not need your full time attention. Your skills should be marketing, administration and strategy. Not looking after the sites on a 24hour basis. You should appoint foreman or supervisors for these functions. Handled well, your week should give you enough time for family and general leisure, time that you would never enjoy working full time in a corporate environment.

Sixth, it does not take mountains of cash to start or operate. Starting costs could only be spent once you have received your first contracts. This is assuming deposits are forthcoming from clients and accounts have been put into place.

Seventh, you can make much more money than you ever dreamed about. Painting contacts can be worth millions of Dollars in any currency. For example, to paint a new high rise building inside and out can exceed one million and a normal size townhouse development could cost $100,000.

3. Why paint contracting businesses fail

There are the usual reasons that fit in with most other businesses; these are a few that are pertinent to our business:

.

- Motivation – or the lack thereof
- Cash flow problems – choosing clients that drag out payments
- Overtrading – taking on more than you can handle
- The economy and therefore the market you are in – a recession will limit your markets, especially new construction projects
- Lack of skills – use this book to increase your skills

Ensuring success
- Motivation – keep up the passion and focus
- Knowing the business - use this book and practice new ideas
- Sticking with it – keep your strategy up to date
- Learning more all the time – become an expert in your field
- Keeping up with trends – use suppliers to learn industry innovations

4. Market trends

Economy

If you stick with refurbishment contracting (more on this subject later), rather than painting new buildings, then general downturns in the economy do not usually affect you much. "New work" or painting done to new buildings is risky, firstly because if there is a downturn in the general building economy and new work begins to dry up and secondly contractors become bad risks.

Refurbishment on the other hand is more prone to an upturn in a tight economy because asset owners turn their attention and cash flow on keeping existing clients rather than building new buildings.

Product development
Suppliers are continuously bringing new products onto the market and frequently these are huge money saving innovations. Examples are paints with wonderful smelling fumes, paints that change colour once they are dry and even paints that glow in the dark. Keep up to speed with technology through your paint suppliers.

Speed of painting
Because of the rise in labour costs internationally, paint contractors try new and innovative methods to cut down on labour and speed up the process. Through product development, many coating systems are now reduced to two coats rather than three, with the primer for example built into the intermediate coat.

Scaffolding methods are increasingly upgraded, as well as application tools such as spray equipment, masking and so on.

Alignments
Many listed or multinational companies are part owners in paint manufacturing companies and often their products are stipulated in the scope of work for the building contracts that are also owned by these multinational companies.

Paint contractors can align themselves with particular manufacturers in order to secure leads.

In Australia, the leading paint manufacturer is a sponsor of a national paint contracting call centre and leads are only given to qualified contractors that are part of this exclusive "club" and have undergone training.

In the USA a leading paint manufacturer has aligned themselves with one of the largest national hardware chains and paint contractors are invited to join this exclusive "club" in order to elicit leads from the hardware chain, generated by the public.

International trends show that clients, paint manufacturers and paint contractors have aligned themselves in order to cut out the opposition.

Find your own niche in your area, and use these alignments to your advantage.

5. What services can you offer

You will often be asked what you do and in response you will answer – paint contracting. Oh, so you paint ships, or oh so you paint lines on the roads. No I paint buildings. Oh so you paint new developments. No I paint buildings that have been painted previously, or yes I paint old buildings, or yes I paint parking lines in car parks.

There are so many different types of paint contracting, you need to find your niche and specialize.

Examples of different types of surfaces that paint contractors paint:

- New buildings
- Refurbishment painting
- Commercial buildings
- Industrial buildings
- Private homes
- Road marking
- Ship painting
- New steelwork coatings
- Pipeline coatings
- Large equipment such as mining
- And so on

Then there are different types of services all together, such as:

- Water proofing
- Damp proofing
- Sealing
- Epoxy coatings
- Polyurethane spraying
- Corrosion control
- Sand blasting
- Needle cleaning
- Plastered coatings
- Earth coats
- And so on

You have to decide where you want to be and focus on these surfaces and services. Most paint contractors paint houses and commercial buildings, new and refurbished. This book will focus on these core markets, even though the principles are the same for waterproofing, damp-proofing and protective coatings.

6. Notes on Waterproofing, Damp-proofing and Protective Coatings

Whilst this manual deals mainly with straight forward paint contracting, the principles can be applied to all of the above and even construction and general contracting.

Marketing – This will differ as to the type of client you will call on. For example:

No	Description	Normal painting	Waterproofing	Damp-proofing	Protective coatings
1	Factories	Y	Y	Y	Y
2	Townhouses	Y	Y	Y	N
3	Commercial	Y	Y	Y	N
4	Government	Y	Y	Y	Y
5	Domestic	Y	Y	Y	N
6	Construction	Y	Y	Y	Y

Costing – This too will differ. With normal painting, the gross profit will be about 40% of turnover, with fairly low rates. With protective coatings, the gross profit is similar, but the rates are much higher, due to the cost of the coatings.

Waterproofing and damp-proofing rates are also much higher, but the gross profit margins are generally much lower (around 20%).

The above costings are only guidelines. You should undertake research and see what your local market can withstand.

7. Mission and vision statement

For any business to succeed, it must know what it is about. It must be able to clearly describe why it is there, and what it is there to achieve. Developing a vision and mission statement is a way of articulating these ideas to yourself, your customers, your employees, and to the world at large.

A Business Vision that Inspires!
If you don't know where you are heading, then you can make any choice and go in any direction (including backwards). The value in knowing your final destination (your vision) is that you can choose to take the specific paths that lead you there. Your action is intentional and keeps you pointed in the right direction.

Vision statements can take many forms. They answer the question: "What will success in the future look like?" Their main purpose is to articulate the "dream" state of the business. If your business could be everything you dreamed of, how would it be? To help you to design your vision statement, try writing your answers to the following questions:

- Why did I start this business?

- When I move on from this business, what do I want to leave behind?

- What am I really providing for my customers beyond products and services?

- If my business could be everything I dreamed, how would it be?

Here is an example of the most well known computer company in the world:

Bill Gates - There will be a personal computer on every desk running Microsoft software.

Once you have created the long-term vision for your business, it creates the context in which all other decisions are made. Your statement should stretch expectations, aspirations, and performance. Without that powerful, attractive, valuable vision, why bother?

A Clear Mission that describes what you do
For any business to succeed, even a business consisting of one individual, it (he/she) needs to know what they're about - what, precisely, it is that they do. The mission statement describes the "what" of your business. It states why your organisation is in business and what you are hoping to achieve.

A typical mission statement contains three components:

1. The overall purpose of your business - what are you trying to achieve, why are you in business

2. What your business does - products and services it provides

3. What's important to your business - the values your business lives by?

Example:

A major pharmaceutical company's mission statement: "*We dedicate ourselves to humanity's quest for longer, healthier, happier lives through innovation in pharmaceutical, consumer and animal health products*".

Purpose:
quest for longer, healthier, happier lives
Business:
pharmaceutical, consumer and animal health products
Values:
innovation

A computer manufacturing company's mission statement - "*With the power of our team of talented people, we are able to provide customers with superb value; high-quality, relevant technology; customised systems; superior service and support; and products and services that are easy to buy and use*".

Purpose: provide customers with superb value technology
Business: high quality, relevant technology, customised systems
Values: superior service and support, easy to buy, easy to use

A well-crafted mission and vision statement becomes the glue that binds the various parts of the business together and drives behavior in your employees. Is it time you had a look at yours?

Both Vision and Mission statements should be short and to the point. The mission statement should be about one line and the Vision about one paragraph.

8. **Strategy – MOST**   A1

    Now that we have covered the Mission statement of the business, let us add to the overall strategy. An overview of strategy is MOST, where:

- **Mission** – as stated in the last section, this needs to be short and to the point. It is the leading statement about the business.
- **Objectives** – These are also short statements about the company's objectives. For example your company could have the following objectives:
  o Financial
  o Marketing
  o Production
  o Human resource management
  o Management information systems

○ Training
○ Safety
○ Quality control
A major listed company could have the following additional objectives:
○ AIDS
○ Research & development
And so on
● **S**trategy – This is the overall business plan, which can change on a regular basis, always allowing for both the Mission and Objectives of the business in mind.

● **T**actics – This is a summary of the business plan,(A2) with a time line. See the summary of MOST on the disc for guidelines.

9. **Seasons and the weather**
   If we are painting indoors it should not really worry us. Mostly this is true, but some paints, especially epoxy paints are susceptible to high humidity levels.

   If you are living in a high humidity environment, you should check the manufacturer's specifications or call their help line. But since most paint contractors are using interior and exterior acrylic paints, which are water based, you should be fine.

   Obviously outside there are other problems that come into play. Rain can always hinder a contract, especially if it comes up suddenly in the afternoon and all your hard work is washed down the drain.

   Wind too, can affect your painting, especially if you are spraying outdoors. It may be that you have to change your prices accordingly, both for paint wastage in windy conditions and make allowances for extra labour.

   You can only work with the elements, not fight them. In high rainfall areas, such as the United Kingdom, paint contractors (and building contractors if the building is new) will cover the entire building with protection, usually plastic sheeting.

   This is obviously costly, but time is often a constraint.

PART 2 – STARTING YOUR BUSINESS

1. How simple it can be
Theoretically starting a paint contracting business can be as simple as the following steps, and you do not even have to use your own money:

- Do some marketing and get a contract
- Receive a deposit from your client
- Buy paint from a paint shop
- Hire a painting crew
- Finish the contract and receive final payment

Yes it can be that easy, buy it is not sustainable. You have no plan, long term labour commitments, or even real knowledge on how to go about real contracting issues.

A real check list to starting your business is as follows: A3

- Start drawing up a business plan A2
- Develop a mission and vision statement
- Register a company name
- Open a legal company
- Open a bank account
- Tend to phone and fax numbers
- Set up a postal address if necessary
- Apply for all the legal requirements such as tax, labour, services and so on
- Organise insurance and public liability
- Secure the services of an accounting officer
- Design a logo for your company name
- Start a web site
- Open one or more paint accounts
- Go on any training your paint companies offer
- Follow all the steps in this book for starting and implementing a paint contracting company
- Interview painters and painting crews
- Decide on what type of paining you would like to do
- Undertake research in your area with regards to potential clients (more under marketing)

- Set up your business premises (usually at home in the beginning is fine)
- Print business cards
- Set out a company profile for marketing purposes and print copies
- Order corporate clothing, both for you and your painters
- Attend to signage, both for your vehicle and sites
- Order the necessary equipment you will need
- Order a small quantity of consumables
- Complete your business plan
- Start marketing

2. **The lifecycle of paint contractors**
   An overview of the cycle of paint contracting is as follows. Note that this cycle is continuous and all functions continue and over-lap:

Marketing	Measure contract	Present quotation	Acceptance	Production	Invoice
Referrals	Meet client	Meeting	Colour selection	Site inspections	Documentation
Advertising	Pricing	Documentation	Site facilities	Quality control	Reference letter
Repeat work	Technical	Specifications	Production schedule	Interim invoices	Referrals
Cold calling	Quotation	Supplier input	Quality plan	Client meetings	Guarantee
Web site			Safety plan	Budget control	How did we perform?
				Hand over	
				Snag list	

Paint contracting is not just as simple as buying paint and applying it to a surface with a brush. It is far more sophisticated than that. The above example shows just what is involved.

If you maintain a professional image the client will:
- Refer you to other clients
- Save money using less paint and labour
- Have less breakdowns
- Generally have less stress and make consistent profit.

- Pay you on time

3. **Working from home**

   The key to running a successful home office is to be organised. Key areas to take note of are the following:

   Work area – generally a small, neat well-organised office in your home will suffice. The following furniture and items would be recommended:

- Your desk & 2 chairs (one for a visitor)
- Shelving for files
- Computer, printer and fax (you can download a free fax number)
- Cell phone
- An answering machine or answering service is recommended
- Keep your production planning board up to date

   Storage area – your garage will work just fine to start. You need a place to store step ladders, paint going to and returning from site and other general equipment.

   Client data base – This is useful for marketing to your clients on an ongoing basis. You can keep your existing and potential clients informed about your activities.

   Administration – Besides keeping accurate records for the Receiver of Revenue, a well organised filing system is necessary. Start with the following files:

- Purchase invoices
- Quotations done
- Stock levels
- Sales reports
- Potential clients
- Invoices and statements
- Completed contracts files
- Suppliers and technical information
- Bank statements

4. An overview of your business

A visual map of your area is useful for planning

Geographical overview

Purchase a detailed map of your area and mount it on a pin board. Select different colour pins so that you can have different codes. After you have identified your 10-20 potential clients or hot spots of potential marketing in each area, use the pins to identify where your potential or existing clients are. The motivation is that you can visualize your business at a glance. This picture of your business can assist with promotions and generally guide you with your daily, monthly and yearly planning.

Contract scheduling board

Set up a large "write and wipe" board on your office wall. Draw in a table of permanent lines, showing the following:

No	Client	Value	Description	Painters	Team	Comments

This is a quick glance of what contracts you have on at any one-time. It assists with planning, shuffling teams around and so on.

Equipment check list

Have a small board showing where all your main capital equipment is at any given time. Once your business starts to grow, you will be amazed at how quickly equipment either disappears or simply gets lost in your own system. Equipment can include step ladders (number them clearly), scaffolding, spray equipment, trailers, high pressure cleaners and so on.

5. Equipment to start your business

This all depends on which market you will target, for example commercial, domestic, industrial or which services you will offer such as painting, protective coatings, waterproofing and so on.

Equipment needed to start your business

No	Description
1	Scaffolding
2	Stepladders
3	Uniforms for staff
4	Uniforms for management
5	Spray gun
6	Hydro-blaster
7	Sandblaster
8	Needle cleaner
9	DFT gauge
10	Damp metre
11	Blast profile
12	Signage
13	Safety equipment
14	Measuring equipment
15	Weather measuring equipment
16	Rope access equipment
17	And so on

Notes:

PART 3 – PAINT MANUFACTURERS

1. Working with your paint supplier

Your lifeline in this business is your paint manufacturer. They determine your account level and therefore your cash flow. They give the go ahead on guarantees if applicable. They take back paint from a site that was not needed. They honor paint failures and guarantees. Paint thicknesses can be checked by the suppliers and therefore if you have applied the correct amount of paint / coats of paint. And so on.

Your paint manufacturer can supply valuable leads and these can come from their regional office, local paint store where you receive your paint from, or even from their sales representative.

2. Specifications

Understanding and writing the correct paint specification can be the difference between success and failure. Basically two things could go wrong:

* You out price yourself with a specification that is an overkill or
* You incorrectly specify and the system fails.

It is prudent to call your paint supplier out to the site, to asses the problem with you. They may have to visit the site anyway, if there is a guarantee to be put in place.

Laying out a professional specification can also impress an analytical client.

Other questions revolve around application. Are cherry pickers or scaffolding needed? Is spraying necessary to speed up the process?

Before you even start with the solution, you have to define the problem. The following table may assist you in asking the correct questions and will assist if you have to approach your paint supplier, then they will have an instant idea of the problem and therefore the solution.

SPECIFICATION QUESTIONS AND NOTES D5

No	Problem	Notes
A	*Environment*	
1	Temperature	*Steel temperature? Solution temperature?*
2	Chemicals	*Acids or corrosive chemicals present*
3	Abrasion	*There are solids in the solution which degrades the coating*
4	Ultraviolet	*The area is exposed directly to the sun and needs UV protection*
5	Is there moisture Present	*Should a moisture curing paint be used that is moisture tolerant*
6	Lighting	*Does the vicinity need extra lighting and therefore a light colour coating should be specified*
7	Time constraint	*Is there a time limit and therefore should build coatings be specified*
8	Other	
B	*Surface*	
1	Surface condition	*Is there old paint, rust, mildew, dust, greases, oils on the surface*
2	Surface type	*Asbestos, steel, wood, concrete*
3	Mill scale	*The presence of mill scale may necessitate the need for sandblasting*
4	Other	
C	*Preparation*	
1	Hand	*Hand cleaning by abrading or wiping*
2	Power tools	*Hand power tools*
3	Water-blasting	*High pressure water-blasting*
4	Sandblasting	*SA2, SA2,5, SA3*
5	Other	
D.	*Coating system*	
1	DFT	*Thickness required*
2	Cost	*Is cost a factor. Is there a life span on the asset?*
3	Other	

3. Accounts

It is crucial to open paint accounts with at least one supplier. This obviously gives you access to decent payment terms, but most often it means you will also receive special discounts as an account holder.

On top of that, you will be on their vendor list, be invited to special events and occasions such as new product launches, golf days and most importantly, you may even be on that special list that gives you leads. These events can often keep you up to date with changing technology in the coatings field.

4. Delivery

Most paint manufacturers will deliver directly either to your offices or even your site. This means you will save money and time, but it also means you should have a lock up store on site.

Most clients will facilitate this requirement. If not, you may have to either cart equipment every day to your site, or hire a small site office.

5. Guarantees

Under certain circumstances, your paint supplier will guarantee not only the paint in the tin, but the paint on the wall. It is not uncommon for a periodic batch of paint to be made, that underperforms on the painted surface.

If you qualify for these types of guarantees, your site will be inspected for correct application procedures. This is a pleasure from both your point of view, knowing your labour is doing their job properly, but also a huge selling point to your client, that they too know, the correct procedures are in place.

If there are any disputes, while the contract is in place or certainly during the guarantee period, your paint supplier will be there to back you up. (Providing your staff has done everything according the correct specifications.)

6. Colour consistency and choice

If you are doing a large paint contract and the same colour has to be coated on most surfaces, batches of paint may differ slightly. This can be very evident to the naked eye.

Paint manufacturers often offer to make the entire batch needed at the same time, but only bill you as and when the paint is taken or delivered. This assists with cash flow, but keeps consistent colour.

Colour choices these days are so advanced, you can purchase a cheap computer disc (or possibly your paint manufacturer will supply one for free). These colour discs offer you the application of taking a photograph of your site or building and changing the colour on the computer, so the final potential outcome can be observed, without opening a tin of paint.

Be aware that the darker the tint of paint is, the more expensive it becomes – especially red, due to the pigments.

7. Training

Paint manufacturers worth their salt, will offer you and your staff free training. This is usually done in the major city centres, at their premises.

They may even offer to send a technical staff member to your site, to assist with on the job training. Take advantage of these offers. Your staff will become more and more professional and save you money.

Notes:

PART 4 – MARKETING

1. Segmenting the markets

There are two different types of markets you should be aware of:

Where you paint

What you paint

Where you paint can be:
- New buildings
- Refurbishment painting
- Commercial buildings
- Industrial buildings
- Private homes
- Road marking
- Ship painting
- New steelwork coatings
- Pipeline coatings
- Large equipment such as mining
- And so on

What you paint or service offer can be:
- Water proofing
- Damp proofing
- Sealing
- Epoxy coatings
- Polyurethane spraying
- Corrosion control
- Sand blasting
- Needle cleaning
- Plastered coatings
- Earth coats

And so on

It is important to decide on what you are offering, which in turn will allow you to focus on the pertinent marketing tools. For example if you decide to paint private homes, it will be very difficult to cold call. And likewise if you decide to paint commercially, it will be silly to do brochure fliers at your local traffic light.

Examples of your services could be:
- We only re-paint private homes
- We only paint new commercial buildings
- We concentrate on re-painting town-house developments
- We offer painting and damp proofing to the entire building industry
- Our specialty is waterproofing and roofs

It is also important to define your markets because your company may have to be geared differently, depending on what you offer or which type of client you paint for.

For example:
- If you are doing new work on commercial buildings, then it is easy to use airless spray equipment.
- Or if you are only painting private homes, the use of scaffolding is unnecessary.
- High rise buildings may require the purchase of swing scaffolding and
- Larger contracts may require that you purchase one or more large trucks to transport labour and equipment.

Many paint contractors have started out with smaller contracts, such as private homes and evolved into the larger, more complicated contracts.

Expertise, confidence and experience will all play a part in deciding which market to concentrate on.

2. **Competitive analysis**
   Competitors can be in the form of either your paint manufacturer or competitive contracting companies.

You may use paint company X and the contract you are tendering on specifies paint company Y. You have a few choices. You can either try and change the specification, in other words offer an alternative, or you have to use company Y. if you do not have an account with them, the chances are you will not receive the best prices.

You will find out quickly, which companies you should have accounts with.

Opposition companies on the other hand are usually easier to deal with. Once you have a rapport with a client, it is rare that price alone is the deciding factor. Most clients will negotiate the contract with you, once they see that your price is in the ball park.

Fly-by-night companies do not last and get caught out. It is amazing how small your industry really is. The best lead is a referral. It is so important to be better than all your opposition. This means PROFFESSIONALISM.

Professionalism in your presentation (yourself, condition of the car you drive, website and especially in your quotation). And then in everything you do on site. From the uniforms of the workers, to cleanliness, to signage and so on.

There is a pyramid of paint contractors in every situation. You want to be at the top of the heap. Not the biggest, but the best. Not the cheapest, but the company that gets ongoing work from a select group of clients.

You

Pick-up-truck brigade

The painters

3. **Research your area**   C5

There is just so much work in the paint contracting field, that it is not worth travelling too far. Research your area and try and fit into what is available.

Typical scenarios can be urban high rise buildings, commercial buildings (not too high, but large areas of factory space) or general domestic homes. You have to adapt your teams and equipment for every market.

Rural areas will not be able to bring in too much work based on proximity of buildings.

Other research can include the types of clients that could potentially give you leads, such as estate agents, property managers, building contractors, managing agents and so on. You will be delighted with just how many potential clients you have in your area.

Researching all aspects of your business is crucial, in order to draw up a useable business plan.

4. **Website**

Professional paint contractors have a simple, but informative website. It acts as a portal into your company, so should be up to date and pertinent. A website can be used for two purposes.

- Getting leads, whereby you activate yourself on the search engines or
- An online brochure of your company for potential clients to see who you are

Buttons on your site could include:

- Home page – outlining a brief overview of what services you offer
- Gallery - Could have photos of contracts. This could include current photos of work in progress as well as a brief history of the contract displayed in the photograph
- Contact and general details, such as professional bodies you belong to, bankers, accountants and so on
- Request a quote – This button could have pertinent details
- Services offered – An overview of exactly what you do
- News –This could outline success stories

- Paint supplier – This could be useful if your chosen supplier is well known. It gives credibility to your company

5. **Sales and marketing control**
   It is essential to keep records and controls of your marketing efforts. The following is a check list with a brief explanation on each point.

- Sales and quotation control book
  Keep this book up to date and allocate quotation numbers to every quotation for future reference.
- Advertising file
  Keep records of all advertising
- Quotation file
  Keep all quotations including rough copies alphabetically in a separate file per year of operation.
- Sales file
  Keep a record of each client, with all their information for marketing opportunities.
- Keep the web site up to date
  Continuously keep your website updated as to company changes.
- Have signs on all contracts displayed outside the building
  This is one of the most powerful marketing tools.
- Keep the pipeline full of quotations
  Without quotations there are no sales and therefore no profits. It is a continuous exercise to give out quotations.
- Keep all staff neatly dressed in their uniforms
  Keep them clean and discard and replace them if they are grubby and well worn.
- Ask for reference letters from your clients
  This can be the most powerful means of marketing.
- Handle all leads quickly and efficiently
  If your response is quick and professional, it tells the prospective client that this contractor should perform in the same manner.
- Monitor leads from advertising and referrals
  Keep a list in your sales file of all leads coming in and where they come from. This can assist with future marketing.
- Sales life cycle
  This is a check list of the actual process how the business runs.
- Quotation and invoice check list
  Check that the following documents are attached to quotations and invoices.

Quotations (What to include)

- Company profile
- Specifications from your paint supplier
- Pricing schedule
- Production schedule (short overview)
- Quality control plan (short overview)
- Safety plan (short overview)
- References with names if possible
- Colour suggestions
- Reference letters
- The contract with terms and conditions

Invoice (What to include)

- Guarantee from you and your paint supplier
- How do you rate our service
- Possible copy of the quality plan

6. The 5 P's of marketing

Marketing plans will always include the "P's" that are pertinent to your company. These are only suggestions and you can add more or change each item to suite your company. The example shows the differences between commercial and industrial painting contractors.

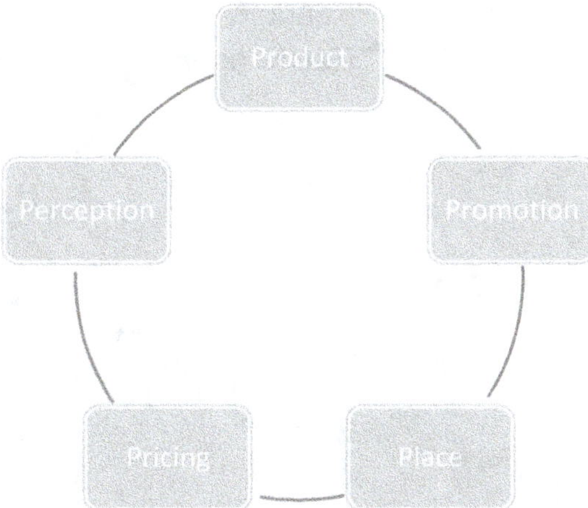

COMMERCIAL PAINTING

Product
- Painting of existing buildings
- Damp proofing
- High pressure washing

Place
- Houses
- Town house complexes
- Blocks of flats
- Commercial buildings
- Churches
- Schools
- Shopping centres

Promotion
- Above the line advertising
- Sign boards
- Banners
- Call centre
- Estate agents
- Knock and drop
- Website
- Email
- Moving bill boards
- In-house representative
- Cold calling
- Referrals
- Leads from suppliers
- External professional bodies
- Tenders

INDUSTRIAL COATINGS

Product
* Protective coatings
* Waterproofing
* Sandblasting

Place
* Factories
* Warehouses
* Electricity supply orgs.
* Harbours
* Hospitals
* Government
* Railways

Promotion
* Cold calling
* Institutions
* Call centre
* Property managers
* Website
* Email
* Sales rep
* Supplier leads
* Tenders
* Estate agents

Perception	Perception
• Professional	* Professional
• Uses the best paint manufacturer	* Best paint supplier
• Quality	* Quality
• Guarantees	* Guarantees
Pricing	Pricing
• Competitive	* Competitive
• Negotiable	* Negotiable
• Receive the best prices from suppliers	* Best supplier prices

7. Promotion explained further

- Above the line advertising – electronic and print   C4

  This form of marketing is usually for building your brand if you are a commercial painter, or generating leads if you paint domestic houses. Either way, it is an expensive way of marketing your business, unless you advertise in the classified section for domestic painting.

- Sign boards

  These can be small boards that you erect in your area (watch out for municipal by-laws) or it can be a very large sign, displayed on your site. Both of these are excellent and cost effective ways of marketing.

- Call centre

  You can either make your own calls or employ someone to do it for you. But if you are painting in the commercial arena, you may only need about ten clients, who keep supplying you with on-going contracts. So whilst this is one of the cheapest and most effective forms of marketing, you will find it is only an initial marketing tool.

  However, some domestic home paint contractors also use call centres effectively. They will get a call centre to call private homes (usually in the evening) and offer a free quotation.

- Estate agents

  Estate agents are also a great way of marketing your business. They work on commission and are at the coal face every day. Offer them a small finder's fee and they will continue to find you work.

- Knock and drop

This is a great way of generating leads or to launch your business. You might want to offer a promotion with a discount or free service, such as high pressure washing the client's roof if they accept the paint contract.

- Email
  Effective if you can obtain lists of clients that you want to target. It is very cheap, but the response is low.
- Moving bill boards
  Very expensive and is used more for brand building. But ALL forms of marketing works in the end of the day.
- In-house sales representative
  Expensive, but if controlled, very effective. The disc has an outline of responsibilities of a representative. F1
- Cold calling
  Most definitely, the best and cheapest form of marketing. Clients want to develop relationships and it is natural for them to know who they are giving large orders to. Pitch up without an appointment and try and see the client. If they are not there, ask if there is someone else you can see. In both instances, drop off a company profile.
- Referrals
  Ask for referrals. You will be surprised. This can be a verbal request or you can ask in writing to rate your company and the service offered.
- Tenders
  This is an easy way to obtain leads for quoting. Note that almost all tenders are for new buildings and the competition will be high and the resulting rates low. It is relatively easy to get onto tender lists with larger building contractors and architects.
- Leads from suppliers
  Develop relationships with your supplier. This might be a loose arrangement, but the larger paint suppliers have approved lists of contractors. You should try and get onto these lists. It is possible you may have to prove yourself over a number of contracts, but it will be worth it in the long run.

Make a matrix similar to the following table, and list your selected markets. Then add the type of marketing you are comfortable with and decide how to approach your clients, with this simple marketing plan.

Market	Advertising	Cold call	Word of mouth
Town house	Yes	Yes	Yes
Commercial	No	Yes	No
Private house	Yes	No	Yes
Factories	No	Yes	Yes
Government	No	Yes	No
New work	No	Yes	No
Industrial	No	Yes	No

- External professional bodies
  There are numerous professional bodies such as:
  ° Paint contractors forum
  ° Paint suppliers associations
  ° Waterproofing associations
  ° Damp proofing associations
  ° Managing agents
  ° Chamber of commerce
  ° Engineering and chemical institutes
  ° Master builders associations
  ° Corrosion organizations

You may have to join and pay an annual fee, but besides receiving leads, you will add credibility to your company portfolio.

8. Time allocation

Initially you should divide your time up as follows.

Sales & marketing	=	60%	
Production on sites	=	30%	First year
Administration	=	10%	

Sales & marketing	=	30%	
Production on sites	=	50%	Second year
Administration	=	20%	

Your time allocated to different functions in your business will differ from the first year in your business, to when it is slightly more mature in the life cycle of your business.

Obviously in the beginning, you will spend more time and effort marketing and later, more time will be spent on sites and controlling production.

9. The quotation pipeline

You need the "QUOTE PIPE LINE" to be filled at all time. This means that once you quote, you have started to fill up one end of an imaginary pipe. The orders for contracts will come out the other end. But as soon as you stop quoting, nothing comes out and therefore there are no profits.

Do not make the silly mistake of getting a few large contracts and pretending you a) have enough money and b) you have enough work. You must keep the quotation pipeline filled at all times.

10. Sales preparation

Make sure you know the proper name of the person you are about to meet. Be formal unless invited to use their Christian name. Be on time and well presented. Present information about your business and what you offer.
 Once you have a brag book or portfolio of contracts completed, take that too.

11. Boundary wall / Roof letter

This is a fun letter that you drop off at a client who has obvious problems, such as a boundary wall or roof that needs painting.

<u>**U R G E N T   M E S S A G E**</u> C2

FROM: *Your Boundary Wall*
TO: *The Home Owner*

<u>*MY CONDITION AND WHAT YOU CAN DO ABOUT IT*</u>

I am sick and my condition is worsening daily. A man from ***Insert your company name*** was here, his name is ***Insert your name*** and he said, he can help to improve my condition, make me feel better and looking good. If my well-being is of some concern to you, please give him a call. He will give a **Free quotation** and handle all necessary steps in a professional manner.

You won't need to buy a hydro-blaster to clean off my loose paint and plaster. You won't need to find out about and buy professional material for crack-filling, bonding liquid, plaster primer and good quality paint to fix me. He will do all that for you and you won't need to take any time off work. Weekends you can still spend with your family and friends instead of painting me.

I am sure your home is important to you and that includes me, your boundary wall. So give ***Insert your name*** at ***Insert your company*** a call. His number is ***Insert your telephone number*** or if he is not busy with somebody else's boundary wall you can reach him at the office number ***Insert an alternative number***, alternatively e-mail him at ***Insert your email address***.

Sincerely
Your Boundary Wall

12. RATE US C3

Thanks for your business and allowing us to be part of your project. By completing this quick survey, you will help us improve our service to you and others. Your comments are appreciated.

1. HOW DO YOU RATE OUR SERVICE

O Excellent   O Very good O Good   O Poor   O Very poor

2. HOW SATISFIED WERE YOU WITH OUR WORK

O Exceeds expectations   O Met expectations O Below expectations

3. DID WE LEAVE YOUR PROPERTY CLEAN AND TIDY

O Yes   O Okay   O No   O Other

4. WERE OUR STAFF FRIENDLY AND KNOWLEDGEABLE

O Yes   O Okay   O No   O Other

5. WOULD YOU RECOMMEND US TO A FRIEND OR BUSINESS ASSOCIATE

O Yes   O No

6. IF YES TO # 5 ABOVE, CAN YOU LIST THE NAMES AND TELEPHONE NUMBERS

____

____

7. HOW CAN WE IMPROVE OUR SERVICE

____

____

13. Company profile C1

The company profile is used for marketing. It can be mailed, emailed, dropped off at a client or even added to a quotation. Your company profile can have the following headings:

- Introduction
- Photographs
- Services offered
- Quality control overview
- Safety features
- History
- Guarantees
- Paint suppliers
- General company details
- Affiliate organizations you belong to
- References – only give client names, not contact details (these can be given on request)
- Payment terms

A company profile can be a substitute for a printed brochure. It can be used for emailing, dropping off with clients and attaching to your quotation. It should include various photographs and be well designed.

Information should be short and to the point. Most people do not have time to read and should be able to quickly glance over the profile and have an understanding of what you are about.

14. Outline for a representative

The following outlines a simple overview of a contract for a representative you may employ.

- Define the market: Factories & industrial complexes
- Salary: XYZ inc vehicle and cell
- Commission;   5%
- Marketing material;   Company profiles to be supplied
- Business cards: Yes, with office number
- Management: Daily reporting
- Control: Weekly meetings
- Sample job description:

To call on industry in the ***Insert your area*** area. To establish contact with factories (or the market you decide to market to) and to find out if the factory needs painting, waterproofing or damp-proofing. Measuring and quotations will be done by the office staff. Some after hours work may be needed if a body corporate meeting is scheduled after hours.

- Commission: Paid back to back with payments received
- Trial: Three months, with 24 hour notice

Notes:

15. Telephone script

Cold calling is hard because of the objections. This telephone script will assist with some of the objections you may receive.

"Hi Mr Jones, this is ***Insert your name*** calling from ***Insert your company name***. We are ***Insert your paint manufacturer's name*** approved paint contractors. (if applicable) Are you looking at painting any part of your house, factory or office soon?"

OBJECTIONS

ANSWER

a. *No*   Do you know anyone who needs a quotation ?

b. *I am painting myself*   Can we offer any advise. We buy paint cheaper than the shops do. Can we offer you a free quote.

c. *I am using a guy referred to me.*   Does he give a Paint guarantee and does his specification cover proper preparation. We hydro-blast everything. Can we give you a free quote.

d. *I am using a local painter.*   All our guys wear uniforms, and have identification. Do you know who you are really using.

e. *I am buying my own paint*   We buy paint cheaper than the shops and our guys are well trained. Let us give you a free quote.

f. *Send me more information*   No problem. I can e-mail, fax or drop off our company profile. Can I drop off a profile when I give you a free quotation.

g. *I will only paint in 6 months time.*   Great, for your budget purposes, can I offer you a free quotation.

16. Keeping photographic records

Photographic records can assist in many ways.

- Marketing to include on your website or company profile
- Disputes if they arise
- Feedback to decision makers if they are unable to visit site
- Methodology for training purposes
- Information for guarantee purposes

17. Corporate clothing

Keeping your company image professional, starts with how your employees look. You may want to differentiate between managers or foreman and the normal painter. Most international painting companies, dress their painters in white two piece coveralls. These should have a simple one colour screen print on the back, with your company name and perhaps logo.

The management could have fancier golf shirts, with the company name and logo embroidered over the pocket or chest area.

Printed caps too, play their part. Not only are they used for branding, but for keeping paint out of the painter's hair.

18. Signage

Small signs similar to the size an estate agent uses, (600 x 400cm), can be put up in your area. The print must be big with one phone number. Make sure you do not infringe on the local by-laws. These signs can be printed cheaply on plastic correx boards.

Larger signs should be printed for display on your sites. These can be in the form of a roll-up banner or a larger sign that is erected on poles if necessary. They can even be temporarily mounted on a wall or even left to stand against a wall.
Often paint suppliers will sponsor these signs if their name is prominently displayed.

Notes:

PART 5 – THE QUOTATION 

It is imperative that the quotation is highly professional, since it is the window to your company. Often the decision maker is someone you may not have met and they will asses you and your company by the presentation and content of your quotation.

It goes without saying, that the quotation should be computer generated and not hand written.

Your quotation should take the form of a template that can be changed for each quotation. D1

1. Overview

The front page should have your logo, company name and company details. It should have the clients name, address and details regarding the quotation, clearly laid out. Also include suppliers and organizations you belong to.

This front page overview sets the scene for the rest of the quotation.
It should also have a short description of the quotation with a reference number.
It is also acceptable to include a short overview of what your company does and stands for.

2. What clients expect

At a quick glance (before it is perused in more detail), a client wants to feel comfortable that this is a professional company. (make sure the binding is neat and possibly include a clear plastic cover).

Note that it is many times more powerful to hand deliver a quotation, rather than emailing or faxing.

The next thing the client does is go straight to the pricing page. This should be a clear table, with all the relevant information well laid out.

No	Description	Qty	Rate	Unit	Total

The price schedule is a bill of quantities.
Definitions:

- *No* is the number of the item mentioned
- *Description* is a brief summary of what is being done
- Qty is the quantity been done
- *Rate* is the actual rate in currency that is being quoted
- *Unit* is the unit specified
- And *total* is the total currency quoted for
- *Sqm* is square metres measured to be painted

No	Description	Qty	Rate	Unit	Total
1	Paint internal walls with acrylic paint to match existing colour	100	sqm	30.00	3000
2	Paint ceiling with white ceiling paint	30	sqm	20.00	600

3. Quotation reference number

Every quotation should have a reference number for ease of finding information at a later date. You can make your own but an easy way to do it is the following:

PC35/11/2012

Where:

- PC is the acronym of your company's name (PC=Paint Company)
- 35 is the is the 35th quotation for that month
- 11 denotes November
- And 2012 the year

So every month a new set of numbers is started, with the first quotation in January of 2012 being:

PC01/01/2012

4. Index - include an index on the second page with page numbers.

5. Analysis of surfaces

This section could end up being your most important legal aid if a dispute arises as to what should have been painted and what should have been left out. It is a summary of exactly what need painting.

No	Area	Surface	Condition	Details
1	Roof	Tiled	Good	Exclude
2	Exterior walls	Plaster	Poor	Paint
3	Doors	Wood	Fair	Exclude

There is no grey area, as to what is quoted on, or what will be painted. This list should be as long as possible, and it should show what will be excluded and what is included.

6. Assessments

If any tests are undertaken on any surfaces, you should record them here.

Different tests
- Levels of moisture in the walls, using a moisture metre.
- Cross hatching (drawing thing parallel lines close together and sticking masking tape over the lines. Then you pull hard and if the paint and or plaster pull's off with it, you have poor plaster and costs will be higher to repair before you paint.
- Solvent test - A solvent test assists in determining the type of paint previously used. This will also help to prevent incompatibility between paint films. Solvent based paints are not normally used for exterior surfaces with the exception of specialized masonry paints which may be over-coated by acrylic.
- Dry film thickness (DFT) – A hand held paint film thickness tester is used to determine the thickness. This can be especially useful to prove that the prescribed amount of paint has been supplied to the walls or surfaces.
- Chalk (rub) test - A poor quality paint or a paint that has been over-tinted will be inclined to chalk when exposed to prolonged ultra violet light (UV). Chalking, which exhibits as a powdery substance on the surface of the paint or fading of the colour, will lead to loss of adhesion if not treated. This test is taken by rubbing the palm of the hand over the surface and if an abnormal amount of powder comes off, then either

the stripping of the surface is required or an intermediate coat of paint (often a solvent based primer is used)

Example

Test	Surface	Result
Moisture test	Exterior walls	An average moisture of 15%
Chalk (rub) test	Exterior walls	No excess powder
Adhesion test	Exterior walls	No evident problems
Dry film thickness test	Exterior walls	Test not taken

7. Scope of work and specifications

This is the exact work that will be undertaken. It lays out the surface area, the problem and the solution. Your paint supplier will be able to give you their specifications to the various painting problems.

Example:

- Metal preparation - All metalwork to be sanded lightly to create a mechanical key for subsequent paint layers as well as smoothing down any previously existing paint runs.
- Painting of metalwork - Paint all metal surfaces with 1 coat of an adhesion promoted enamel, formulated to a tough gloss finish. It is non-yellowing, flexible and very U.V. resistant. Excellent for gutters, windows, doors, etc, applied to a Dry Film Thickness of not less than 25 microns.

8. Paint supplier recommendations and site inspection

Often paint suppliers will go to site even before you have received an order, to assist with technical problems and writing a specification for all the work to be undertaken.

This report should be attached to your quotation. It could also form part of the paint supplier guarantee if it is requested.

9. Company details

This is a list of details where you should be transparent with the following information:

- General details, including website, email, fax and telephone numbers and addresses
- Bank details
- Auditors
- Affiliate organizations
- Legal numbers such as tax and employee registration numbers

10. References

This select reference list is your chance to brag. You can list the following information:

No	Client	Value	Date	Type
1	XYZ Hospital	100,000	2011	Painting to exterior walls
2	Mr Jones	5,000	2011	Painting outside of house

11. Terms and conditions

These terms and conditions should be standard and let the client know exactly what is needed from their side and what you will be supplying.

- Payment – exactly how payment will work
- Site facilities – you need water, electricity, lock up storage and so on
- Liability – your insurance and liability indemnity
- Quality control procedures
- Site access – you need unhindered reasonable site access
- Completion – when the site will be deemed complete
- Guarantees

A full example of the quotation is in a template form on the disc. D1

PART 6 – SERVICE CONTRACT & GUARANTEE 

1. **Service contract** D4

   This is your signed order. It should be short (2 pages) and have all the relevant information.

   - Names of both parties
   - Details of work to be undertaken
   - Exactly how payment will be paid. Deposit if applicable, interim invoices and final payment on completion after snag (problem areas) have been attended to.
   - Signature section with place for witnesses
   - Terms and conditions as laid out in part 5, section 11

2. **Guarantee** D3

   This is a very contentious area and you should be particularly careful.

   The best guarantee is a back-to-back one from your paint supplier. These also tend to vary:
   - Full term i.e. The paint is guaranteed on the walls for 5 years.
   - Reducing i.e. The paint is guaranteed on the walls for 5 years, reducing by 20% per year.

   Many paint manufacturers will not entertain a guarantee of their paint on the wall, but rather only in the tin and then until it is opened.

   Most will only guarantee a contract if you as the paint contractor is approved by them. This means you may have to be assessed under certain criteria, but it is well worth it in the long run.

   But the client expects some sort of guarantee.

   The most common, is the painting contract will be guaranteed for a one year period, or full season of all weather conditions. If your workmanship is up to scratch and your painting specification is correct, this need not be an issue.

Most contracts fail because of poor preparation. It is so important to work according to a quality system, to ensure this does not happen. (more under production)

Important points to be covered in a guarantee:
- The parties concerned
- Inspections carried out on site
- Products used
- The exact surface to be guaranteed (it is possible that you offer a guarantee at a particular address, but only part of the building has been painted and guaranteed)
- Inclusions or what you are offering a guarantee on
- Exclusions are areas you are not offering a guarantee on (often trim-work or steel surfaces like windows an so on). Also acts of God or terror and most importantly, defective materials.

3. A guarantee template is on the disc.   D3

4. **How the paint manufacturers play their role**
    If a paint manufacturer offers to guarantee a contract, not only does the client have peace of mind, but so do you. They undertake site inspections that are often not pre-arranged.

    Often photographic records are taken and wet and dry film paint applications are recorded, to ensure the correct amount of paint is been applied to the walls.

    The site inspection will normally record only one specific area of the contract and if, in the future there is a problem, then they will test the previously tested areas.

    This ensures that the correct paint was applied and the correct degradation has taken place. Only then will they look at the affected areas and test these areas.
    Most often it is an application failure and also happens in the first year.
    The client will the have full recourse on you and you your company.

PART 7 – MANAGEMENT INFORMATION SYSTEMS

1. How to record and file information

Even though we are living in a computerised society, it is important to keep hard copies of your records. When you measure a contract, it is done with a pad and pen. You physically draw the building and take notes.

Then you do the calculations and work the actual costs out. These too, should be kept as a hard copy in a file.

You may also take colour scrapings from a wall or add brochures or leaflets from the site. There may be many items you will want to file.

These records, along with the hard copy of the quotation, should be kept in files marked quotations. You will be surprised how often in the future you refer to these notes. You may quote today and receive an order in a year's time. We do tend to forget.

2. Contract completed records

At the same time, once a contract has been completed, all the records need to be recorded. There are many instances in the future that you may need to refer to a completed contract's records:

- Invoice disputes
- The client may ask what the colour code on the walls are, 2 or 3 years later
- Guarantee purposes
- Actual profit calculations
- Theft queries
- Tax audits
- And so on

PART 8 – TRAINING

1. Training – In-house

Since you are doing your own marketing, your training is confined to the technical aspects of paint contracting. It is critical to keep up with ongoing training programs for your staff.

Your clients and suppliers will see the benefits, as will you, on your bottom line. Training should include:

- Responsible painting practice
- Correct surface preparation techniques
- General housekeeping
- Cleaning up after a days painting and after your site has been completed
- Storing paint safely on site and at your offices
- Transporting paint responsibly
- Getting rid of old paint
- Painting techniques, including:
    - Surface preparation
    - Stripping
    - Priming
    - General specifications
    - Acrylics
    - Enamels
    - Wood paints and varnishes
    - Parapet wall sealing
    - Trim work
    - Roofs

It is imperative that you understand all the different painting techniques and specifications that are available. There are many sources of information available on painting, including your paint manufacturer, the internet, books and outsourced training companies.

2. **Training – Paint suppliers**

    All the professional paint suppliers offer in house and on site training to staff. Send your foreman and managers to the longer courses and ask your paint supplier to visit your site with in-situ training.

3. **Training - Safety**

    Safety training must be kept up to date and relevant to what your company's services are. For example if you are dealing with asbestos roofs, then you need a certificate that allows your staff to work in this environment.

    Also if you are painting solvent based paints in an enclosed area such as a tank, safety issues are very different to painting the walls of a house.

    See section G on the CD, which deals with safety in more depth.

    Notes:

PART 9 – COSTING

1. How to estimate a contract

Estimating or costing a contract has a specific methodology and you should never take a short cut. Once an order has been accepted from a client, it is very difficult to go back and say you have either measured incorrectly, or your calculations are wrong.

Methodology overview:
Site measuring

- Check the scope of work with the client
- Take a short walk around the site to familiarize yourself
- Draw a plan view of the building
- Measure the site with a measuring wheel and tape measure
- Use the same codes or references when taking notes (see codes below)
- Take photographs liberally
- Take samples of paint or plaster if necessary
- Undertake tests if necessary (moisture, adhesion and so on)

Office work

- Draw up a bill of quantities (description, quantity, unit, rate & total)
- Calculate all the measurements & fill the information in the bill of quantities
- If you know your rates then fill them in on the BOQ
- If the specification is unknown, then deal with your paint manufacturer for the correct painting systems
- Make sure you have the correct paint prices and spreading rates of the paint
- Calculate the rates
- Using your quotation template, fill in the pertinent data for the particular quotation
- Add photographs if necessary
- Add tests undertaken
- Add your company profile if it is a new client
- Add your paint manufacturers report if they undertook a site inspection

2. Symbols for costing and quoting

Every industry has its own unique reference codes. Herewith are a few to assist in the painting industry.

No	Symbol	Definition	Description
1	S/S	Single story building	Each story is 3,2 m high
2	D/S	Double story building	2 stories high
3	↑	Vertical height	The actual height of a wall or structure
4	→	Horizontal length	The length of a wall or surface
5	⬭	Diameter	Diameter of a circular structure
6	Qty	Quantity	How many of each item
7	Off	How many	How many individual items
8	Rate	Amount	The currency amount to be charged
9	Unit	Unit	The unit of measure e.g. Square metres
10	Sqm	Square metres	The area of a flat surface
11	Lm	Linear metres	The length of a structure
12	xxxxx	Damp	There is damp in this area
13	d/p	Down pipe	A down pipe at this corner of the building
14	pc	Preliminary cost	The budget amount
15	Um	Micron	1000th of a millimetre
16	DFT	Dry film thickness	Thickness of dried paint
17	WFT	Wet film thickness	Thickness of wet applied paint
18	Comb	WFT gauge	Small hand held gauge to measure WFT
19	WP	Waterproofing	Waterproofing needed in this area

3. Tools for costing

When you have committed to go all the way out to the site or building, then the following tools should always be on hand.

- Measuring wheel
- Tape measure (5 metres long). This length assists in measuring heights
- Pad and pen
- Water bottle if the site take hours of walking to measure
- Cap and suntan cream
- Digital camera
- Moisture metre
- Hard clip board to hold your pad of blank paper
- Small roll of masking tape to do cross hatching (adhesion test)
- Small pen knife to take scrapings

4. Formulae's to assist with costing

Herewith are a few of the common formulas that you may find helpful:

1	Area of a square	Length x breadth
2	Area of a rectangle	Length x breadth
3	Area of a triangle	Half base x height
4	Area of a circle	$A = \pi r^2$
5	Circumference of a circle	$C = 2\pi r$

5. Quotation check list  D2

It is easy to forget all the different areas that have to be inspected and measured on site. The following check list will assist:

Surface	Description	Surface	Description
Exterior		**Roofs**	
Walls		IBR	
Dark colour		Tiled	
Rough plaster		Flat	
Smooth plaster		Corrugated	
		Parupets	
Windows		Waterproofing	

Steel		Pitched	
Wood		Flashings	
Aluminium		Gullies	
Putty		Drainage	
Other items		**Boundary wall**	
Downpipes		Painting	
Gutters		Damp on parapets	
Facias		Gates	
Cracks		Cracks	
Sprockets		Expansion joints	
Balustrades		Concrete	
Plants		Wood	
Expansion joints		Pre-cast	
		Palisade	
Interior			
Walls		**Other areas**	
Doors		Guard house	
Frames		Pool area	
Ceilings		Electricity supply	
Skirting		Front gate	
Cupboard doors		Garage doors	
Move furniture		Storm water	
Damp		**Staircases**	
Rising		Seal edges	
Lateral		Sealer	
Stripping needed			
Injection		**Floors**	
-		Epoxy	
Waterproofing		Enamel	
Torch on / liquid			
Drains		**Corrosion**	
Slope of roof		Needs SA2, SA2,5	
Up-stands		Spark problems	
Bolts / side laps		Water-blasting	

6. Overview of costing

There are two ways to determine the cost of a project to be painted.

- Determine the total cost of paint required and add it to the estimated amount of labour. Then add any incidental products. You now have the total cost, before profits. Add your expected profits and the total is what you would charge to paint that particular structure or building.
- Or, calculate the area that needs to be painted. Then calculate the spread rate of the paint per litre, multiplied by the cost of the paint per litre. Add to that the amount of labour needed per square metre. Then add incidental products and profit. This gives a total of all costs per square metre. Multiply by the total area that needs to be painted.

We will be working with the latter method of costing. i.e. Calculating a square metre rate multiplied by the total amount of square metres that needs painting.

7. Dry and wet film thickness

Before we can start understanding how to calculate the paint required, we need to understand Dry Film Thickness (DFT) and Wet Film Thickness (WFT).

All paint has solids and liquids as part of its chemical make-up. Water based paint, such as acrylic PVA, has water as the liquid carrier and solvent based paint has solvents, such as enamels.

Once paint has been applied to a surface, the solids stay behind and the water or solvents evaporate.

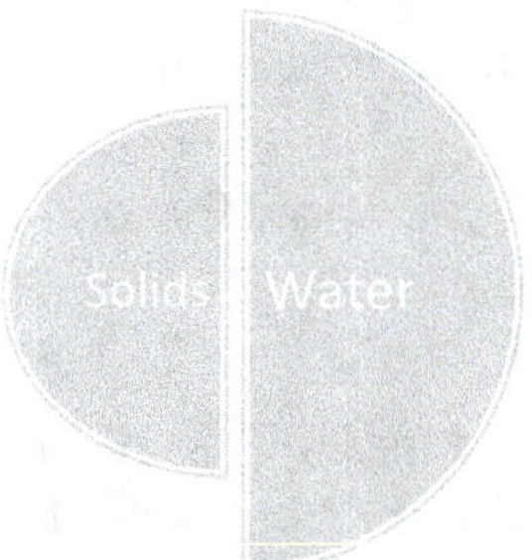

Water based paint will have more water to evaporate

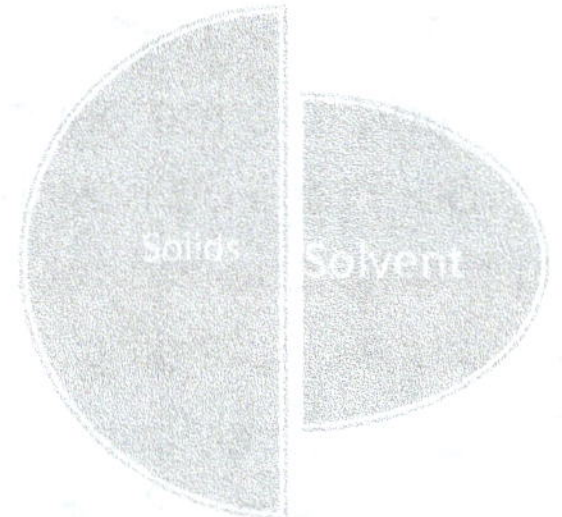

Epoxy paints have fewer solvents to evaporate

The amount of paint left behind is measured in microns. 1mm equals 1000microns. To show how thin paint is applied to a surface, a normal coat of exterior acrylic is applied at about 25-40 microns per coat (very, very thin). But this shows how strong paint is and if cheap paint is purchased, it will not have all the prerequisites for the paint to last long.

To measure WFT, a small hand held devise is used, called a comb. It is stuck into the wet paint and shows, through different calibrations, the WFT of the paint. Once the solvent or water has evaporated, only the solids will be left behind.

The thickness of the paint is measured as DFT or dry film thickness. This is measured with a hand held microscope, which etches itself into the dry paint on the surface and shows each coat of paint ever applied to that surface and its thickness in microns.

DFT is calculated to be applied by a normal brush or roller over one coat of application.

Each paint has a specific formulae to work out the difference of WFT to DFT. Because some paints as shown above, have more solvents than others, it means that the WFT and the DFT will differ due to their chemical make up.

Most paint containers or technical data sheets will show the difference.

Example:
A PVA acrylic is applied at 50 microns WFT and its DFT is 25 microns. This means that 50% of the solvents have evaporated or "flashed off".

8. Material spread rate

Now we understand paint thicknesses, we can calculate material spread rates. All paint containers and paint data sheets will tell you the spread rate per litre of paint and how many microns it will dry at (DFT).

Example:
If a litre of paint costs $10 and the spread rate is 10 litres per square metre and the DFT is 25-40microns. Calculate the rate per square metre.

$$\text{Rate of paint per sqm} = \frac{cost\ per\ litre}{spread\ rate}$$

$$\text{Rate of paint per sqm} = \frac{10}{10}$$

Rate of paint per sqm = $1-00 per square metre

So it will cost $1-00 to paint this particular paint per square metre. If there were 1000 square metres, then the cost would be 1000sqm X $1-00 = $1000.

If however the required DFT was 50-80 microns, you would have to apply double the amount of paint. But with a normal roller or paint brush, this paint will only go on at half the required amount, so you will need to apply two coats of paint.

9. Labour calculations

A man costs the company xyz per month, day or hour. The big question is, how many square metres can one man paint in one day, which will give us the answer of what the labour rate is per square metre.

The following estimate is a guideline and allowances must be made for weather, heights and other abnormal circumstances.

A man should paint about 100sqm per day on a single story building, using a short ladder. If he paints multi-story buildings on scaffolding, the rate could come down as low as 25sqm per day.

If a man is therefore paid $100 per day and he paints 100 sqm per day, the formulae for a labour rate is:

$$\text{Labour rate} = \frac{cost\ per\ day}{sqm\ per\ day\ he\ can\ paint}$$

$$\text{Labour rate} = \frac{100}{100}$$

Labour rate = $1-00 per square metre

Man days
Labour can be laid out in man days, i.e. how many days will it take to complete that particular contract and with how many painters.

Efficiency varies with
- The degree of difficulty of preparation and application
- Working at ground level or on scaffolding
- Contract variables
- Substrates which vary from rough to smooth
- Working conditions

The most reliable basis for determining labour efficiencies would be your own records which you should update from time to time. The following estimates are working on the ground floor of a normal building:

Description	Sqm per worker per day
Hydro blasting	100
Wire brushing	25
Sanding	15
Patch priming	30
Rolling water based paint	120
Airless spraying water-based paint	400
Sandblasting	25
Rolling solvent based paint	80
Brushing solvent based paint	50
Spaying solvent based paint	200

Examples of calculating man days to undertake various functions are as follows on a 1000sqm surface area of a building:

- Hydro blasting $\frac{1000}{100}$ = 10 man days. 2 Men = 5 days for completion

- Sanding $\frac{1000}{15}$ = 67 days. 10 Men =6,7 days for completion
- Airless spraying $\frac{1000}{400}$ = 2,5 days

10. Case study

Assumptions
- Paint the exterior of a house
- 1000sqm contract (measured on site)
- Painters are paid $100 per day

Specification
- Prepare all walls by filling cracks and washing the walls down with water
- Prime all walls with Abc primer at 25-40 microns DFT
- Paint 2 coats of Xyz acrylic paint at 25-40 microns DFT

Paint technical data
- Abc primer spread rate is 8sqm / litre and the price is $100 per drum of 20 litres
- Xyz acrylic spread rate is 10sqm / litre and the price is $150 per drum of 20 litres

Calculations
Materials
- Abc primer - $100 for a 20 litre drum divided by 20 litres = $5-00 per litre, divided by 8sqm/litre = $0.63 per square metre. (this means it costs 63 cents per square metre to paint one coat of primer on the wall)
- Xyz acrylic paint - $150 for a 20 litre drum divided by 20 litres = $7-50 per litre, divided by 10sqm/litre = $0.75 per square metre. (this means it costs 75 cents per square metre to paint one coat of acrylic paint on the wall)
- Crack repair materials, sand paper and so on. An easy way is to calculate, is to allocate about 5%of the total material costs for incidentals, unless it is evident that it is more.

Labour

- Painters are paid $100 per day and can paint 100sqm per day. Therefore the cost of applying 1sqm to the wall is $1-00
- Preparation usually takes about the same amount of time it takes to paint a full coat of paint to the walls, including washing. (in this instance $1-00 per sqm)

Item	Description	Qty	Unit	Rate	Sub-total	Total
Materials	Abc primer	1000	sqm	0-63	630-00	
	Xyz acrylic – 1st coat	1000	sqm	0-75	750-00	
	Xyz acrylic – 2nd coat	1000	sqm	0-75	750-00	
					2130-00	2130-00
	Incidentals @ 5%					106-50
Labour	Preparation	1000	sqm	1-00	1000	
	Primer	1000	sqm	1-00	1000	
	1st coat acrylic	1000	sqm	1-00	1000	
	2nd coat acrylic	1000	sqm	1-00	1000	4000-00
	Sub-total					6236-50
	Profit at 80%					4989-20
	Total					11225-70

Notes:

- Profit margins can be adjusted to how much work you have, how competitive the environment is as well as many other factors.
- Most of the work you undertake will be the same. You will therefore use similar rates in almost all your quotations. It is however, important to understand how to calculate the rates and be able to adjust your prices, depending on the four main input costs:

o Materials or paint

o Labour

o Incidentals

o Profit

- Other items to cost in may be:
○ Hire of equipment
○Transport to site if it far
○Scaffolding costs (hire and erection)
○Specialists

- Overheads such as transport, head office salaries, insurance, marketing, telephones, stationary and so on will be deducted off your profit, which is called Gross profit. Once other items such as tax and interest are deducted, then this profit is called net profit after tax and interest. (more under the finance section)

11. Measuring plans / blue prints

- Unroll the blueprint onto a flat surface. Tape or weight the edge so it does not roll up when measuring.
- Find the scale of the drawing. Blueprints will have a block of information, usually in one corner or along one side of each page, that shows the name of the firm or person who drew them, the date and revision information, the name of the project, the title of the page, the page number and the total number of pages in the drawing set. Here is where you will find the scale for the drawings on the page.
- Choose a scaled ruler that accurately matches the scale of the drawing. Triangular architectural or engineering rulers offer many scales on their surfaces and are very accurate. Highly accurate longer flat rulers with the most popular scales are also available. Scale fans include rulers with all the most popular scales but are relatively short and hard to work with for detailed measurements. Rolling scales that trace over drawings, accumulate dimensions, and make calculations may be okay for estimators but are not suitable for detail work.
- Lay the proper scale next to the item on the drawing and take the measurement. The scale will translate for you. As an example, a 1mm (millimeter) = 1 metre architect scale will have markings that increase by 1 metre every 1 millimetre; a 3 metre wall is represented by a 3-centimetre length, if measured with a conventional ruler.
- Enter your scaled measurements into a calculator to determine length or circumference; area in square metres; or volume of objects, property plots, or rooms.

12. Advanced average spreading rate

Normal brush and roller application formulae is as follows:

ASR = VS x 10 X utilization

$\qquad$ (1,3 x DFT) + (0,5 x P)

Definitions:

ASR $\qquad$ Average spreading rate

VS $\qquad$ Volume solids

DFT $\qquad$ Fry film thickness

Utilisation $\qquad$ A factor which takes into account the variable "losses" involved in converting paint in the container to a DFT on the chosen surface.

- Losses include: filling of profile, absorption into substrate, wastage (left on roller, spillage, left in container, overspray), overlaps, excessive build up, sags and so on.
- Utilisation for brush and roller: approx 0,9, spraying: approx 0,7

(varies with profile, absorption, applicators skill etc)

- P $\qquad$ Profile of surface in microns

Example:

ASR = VS X 10 X utilisation

$\qquad$ (1,3 x DFT) + (0,5 x P)

ASR = 80 X 10 X 0,9

$\qquad$ (1,3 x 25) + (0,5 x 30)

ASR = 80 X 10 X 0,9

$\qquad$ (1,3 x 25) + (0,5 x 30)

ASR = <u>720</u>

$$\qquad (32,5) + (15)$$

ASR = 15 SQM / litre

Because you're not painting a sheet of perfectly smooth glass, other factors affect this theoretical coverage rate.

It just shows how many factors you have to take into account when costing. Volume solids in paint is probably the most important factor to deal with. But note the other factors such as overspray, surface configuration, blast profile, painter experience and product losses play an important role as well.

Application methods can produce losses ranging from 5% to more than 50%.

13. Additional costing information

- Guide to surface profiles

○ Cement plaster

    ♦ Steel trowel: 20 microns

    ♦ Wood trowel: 30 microns

    ♦ Rough plaster: 50 microns

○ Smooth sealed primed surfaces: 1 micron

○ Painted smooth cement plaster: 5 microns

Profiles and porosity will vary depending on the application and drying conditions and composition of the plaster.

- Conversion of DFT to WFT

Wet film thickness (WFT) in microns = <u>DFT (microns) x 100</u>

$$\text{VS\%}$$

Example:

Acrylic has VS = 40%. What WFT must be applied to achieve 25 microns DFT?

WFT required = $\frac{25}{40}$ x 100 = 62,5 microns

14. Measuring a building
  - Measure all the walls and calculate the total area of each wall. (height X width = area)
  - Add up the area of all walls
  - Calculate the area of all doors openings, windows or areas that do not need to be painted. (ignore the very small areas)
  - Subtract the areas above that do not need painting. This leaves you with the area that needs to be painted
  - Ceilings and floors are simply length X breadth

Notes:

PART 10 – PRODUCTION

1. Budgeting the contract

Planning a paint contract involves many items, but the main one is doing a financial budget. Did you make a profit or loss? You may have many different types of contracts on the go at the same time. Is spraying roofs making more money than painting floors?

With this type of information, you can steer your business into profitable areas, by changing things like marketing, the type of equipment you use and the type of labour you hire.

Budget
Lay out a budget for the contract, which includes labour, paint, incidentals and hire expenses.

Budget costing example　　B3

No	Description	Qty	Unit	Rate	Sub-Total	Total	Actual costs	Variance %
A	PAINT							
1	Primer	2	20litre	$100	$200			
2	Acrylic	6	20litre	$150	$900	$1100		
B	LABOUR							
1	Preparation	4	Man days	$100	$400			
2	Primer	2	Man days	$100	$200			
3	1st Coat	2	Man days	$100	$200			
4	2nd Coat	2	Man days	$100	$200	$1000		
C	INCIDENTALS							

						$55	$55		
	5% Paint costs								
D	HIRING COSTS								
	Scaffolding	1	3m tower	$800	$800	$800			
E	SUB-TOTAL						$2955		
F	SALE						$5000		
G	PROFIT						$2045		

Monitor the actual expenses (B2) and compare them to the budgets. This is one of the most crucial exercises to do, while running a successful paint contracting company. This information will give you the edge, when at a moments notice you may have to negotiate a potential contract.

Also, monitoring all the expenses sends a message to your staff and suppliers. It is good practice.

2. **Production schedule** B4

   Your company production schedule should be on a write and wipe board in your office in order to plan your contracts. This is an example of what it could look like. Other information could be added, such as which team, the value of the contract, the area, a description of the contract and so on.

No	Description	Weeks	1	2	3	4	5	6	7	8	9	10	11	12
1	House					←						→		
2	Dog parlor			←		→								
3	Church				←								→	
5	Sports club										←			→

But a production schedule for a particular client is planned and printed on from your computer.

It involves only that particular contract and instead of weeks as in the example above, it often shows days, if the contract is a short one, such as a house. It could also be that you have multiple schedules if the sites have multiple buildings.

No	Description	Days	1	2	3	4	5	6	7	8	9	10	11	12
1	Prepare walls													
2	Primer													
3	1st Coat													
5	2nd Coat													

3. **Check list when starting a contract**   B6

   You may have more items that you want to add.

No	Description	Tick
1	Specification on site	
2	Contract in place and signed	
3	Guarantee in place – paint supplier	
4	Paint supplier technical contacted	
5	Site register	
6	Budgets done	
7	Quality documents	
8	Production schedule	
9	Client regular meetings set up	
10	Site storage organised	
11	Signs outside the site for marketing	
12	Toilet facilities organized for the labourers	
13	Water access	
14	Electricity access	
15	Wages negotiated if necessary	
16	Bonuses negotiated if necessary	
17	Safety system in place	
18	Safety officer appointed in writing	
19	Scaffolding permits in writing	
20	Trash bins for rubbish organized	
21	Necessary small tools on site	

| 22 | Step ladders on site | |
| 23 | Staff uniforms handed out | |

4. **Check list when completing a contract**   ◢B7

You may have more items that you want to add.

No	Description	Tick
1	Guarantee in place	
2	Site cleaned	
3	Actual costing up to date with variances	
4	Quality documents completed and filed	
5	Signs outside premises removed	
6	Toilet facilities removed	
7	Rubbish bins removed	
8	Ladders, scaffolding and tools removed	
9	Final invoices in place	

5. **Site control paperwork**

It is crucial to have all the necessary paperwork on hand. Open two new files, one for the office and one for the actual site.

The office file should contain the following: ◢B1

- The quotation
- The rough notes when measuring up
- The specification
- Budgets
- Actual expenses
- Production schedule
- Any additional information
- Delivery notes

The site file should contain the following:

- The scope of work
- Staff site register
- Quality form and plan
- Production schedule

Completed contracts file:
This should be all completed contracts, filed alphabetically for future reference. It should contain all the information, including guarantees, contracts and so on. It is possible that some contract completed files, are so thick, they may have to be filed in boxes.

6. Site preparation

The following items are things that normally have to be done to prepare a site for work. The previous site check list can be used in conjunction with this site preparation.

- Site hut or secure area for storage
  Hire a site hut if you feel the contract will carry on for a long period of time. Alternatively, ask the client for permission for storage space.
- Electricity
  If electricity is needed, ask the client up front for this facility. If necessary, hire a generator.
- Water
  Always have a spare collection of hosepipe connections for different taps. Never use fire hydrants.
- Ablutions
  Keep ablution facilities clean and supply toilet paper, soap and so on.
- Rubble removable
  It may be necessary to hire a skip to cart away rubble. Take all rubbish to a recognised dump.
- Parking
  Be mindful of parking and do not block right of way traffic.
- Inspections
  Make progress inspections with the client and suppliers routine.
- Production board
  Have a write and wipe board to project and show at a glance which sites you have coming up to assist in the planning of contracts. Keep it up to date.
- Sub-contractors
  Keep control of all sub-contractors and their contracts.
- Site register
  In the site file, keep a daily record of all staff, for actual costing records.
- Quality plan

A quality plan is a critical part of site control. Using the quality plan properly will save money. (See the quality plan section).

- Guarantee

Keep records of all guarantees in the contracts completed file for future use.

- Production schedule

Plan every contract using the production schedule. Write in the scope of work for the contract and across the top put in a time line. Keep this schedule up to date at all times.

- Meetings

Regular meetings with minutes are crucial. Put everything in writing, especially extras to the contract so no arguments can be made later.

The following meetings should be held on a regular basis.
- Staff meetings at least twice a year to assess their happiness in the work place.
- Monthly accounting meetings with your accounting officer.
- Weekly internal production meetings, or daily as may be required.
- Weekly site meetings with your client.

7. Doing the painting

- Use the correct tools
- Keep plenty of drop sheets or plastic covers on hand to avoid paint spillages onto clean surfaces.

8. Quality control

A quality system is very simple and saves money. Essentially it monitors the exact scope of work you undertake and keeps records. For example, the scope of work could be as follows:

No	Description
1	Hydro-blast all external walls
2	Patch prime and fix cracks
3	Apply one coat of primer to walls
4	Apply first coat of acrylic paint to walls
5	Apply second coat of acrylic paint to walls

How do you know the walls have been properly hydro-blasted, or hydro-blasted at all? How do you know that the second coat of paint has been applied?

A quality plan allows a system to monitor these activities. It also gives peace of mind to the client, yourself and the paint supplier who may be giving you a guarantee. (Even though they will do their own monitoring).

A quality plan will include the following:

- Name of the client
- Date
- Name of the project
- The full scope of work
- The organisations who will sign off each stage
- Place for date and signature of each sign-off stage
- The final approval of each person tasked with inspecting each stage
- A remarks column

Quality plan B5

No	Description	Paint Supplier	Client	QC Company	Your Company	Comments
		Sig/date	Sig/date	Sig/date	Sig/date	
1						
2						
3						
4						
5						
6						
7						
8						
	Approved by	Paint Supplier	Client	QC Company	Your Company	
	Name					
	Position					
	Date					
	Signature					

Appointing an external quality control company is a good move for all stakeholders. Clients and suppliers see extra eyes on site as a huge bonus. They have peace of mind that the job is being done properly.

You as the owner of the contracting company should see the extra inspections as positive and a mechanism for saving money.

- The disc has the following templates to assist with on site quality control:
- 13 Final release certificate
- 14 Inspection & test report
- 15 Psychometric data: Relative Humidity
- 16 Psychometric data: Steel Temp

9. Staff site register

A simple staff register will avoid discrepancies when it comes to who was on site and when. Especially when you have multiple sites, sub-contractors and sites where identification is required.

On multiple sites, it is difficult to know who was where and when. Costing the contract as well as pay day is much easier if all staff sign in on a daily basis. Larger contracting companies such as construction sites, have mobile electronic devices for monitoring staff.

Sub-contractors often have a way of asking for more money, after the contract has been successfully negotiated. The price for the contract may have been set up front, as well as the amount of painters the sub-contractor allows for the site. A site register, even for them is important, in order to avoid confusion at the end.

Often government sites or sites where a high level of security or safety is concerned, insist on every painter having identification. They may also insist on a site register on a daily basis.

Staff site register B8

No	Name	Day1	Day2	Day3	Day 4	Day 5	Day 6	Day 7

10. Visitors register B9

A simple A5 exercise book is all you need for a visitors register. It records every official visit to site. It monitors yourself, your management, suppliers, independent inspectors but also the client or representative themselves.

It can happen that the client complains that you as the owner is never on site. A simple referral to the site register book will confirm the opposite.

It also shows both you and the client, how often your supplier is on site, monitoring the guarantee that was possibly put into place.

11. House keeping

Good housekeeping or tidiness is good manners and good practice.

- Toilets – clean, toilet paper, soap
- General site – old tins, sandpaper, paint flakes
- Washing equipment – use drains or basins (water based paint)
- Solvents – take from site and dispense with your paint supplier
- Uniforms – shoes, t-shirts, pants – keep neat and clean
- Attitude – noise, smiling, dealing with customers
- Smoking – butts, near to clients is a no-no
- Lunch and tea – find a quite place that no one can see you and clean up
- Parking bays – stick to the bays given to you
- Site hut or area - site file, site register with all visitors signed in, queries, paint invoices and paper work. Keep the site hut or area clean

12. The site clean-up

- Ensure that all tapes have been removed
- Using a scraper, carefully remove all dry drops of paint from windowsills and outside paved areas
- Replace all hardware, doors, light switches, plug covers and re-hang light fittings
- Once drop sheets have been folded up from inside painting, unfold them outside and shake them out. This will help to avoid a mess on your next contract
- Small dried paint clots on carpets can be cut off using scissors
- Clean all tools properly, even if it means doing so back at your office and check for safety problems such as electrical fittings
- Clean brushes straight after use. Dried paint will render brushes and rollers as un-useable
- Use water to clean equipment that used water-based paint
- Use the correct brush cleaner for oil-based paint cleaning
- Write notes on paint tins that you want to keep for touch-ups on a contract.
- Re-use mineral turpentine and store in a tight container
- Rather than throwing toxic solvents down drains, rather let them evaporate
- Let rags and papers that have been soaked in solvents dry out before transporting them. They can combust spontaneously

13. Stock control

You can lose money easily if stock control is not tightly controlled.

- Equipment

Keep a record of all equipment such as tools, ladders, scaffolding and so on. (you need this for regular safety inspections anyway). Keep a check where all your equipment is at all times. It is so easy for equipment to be left behind, or other contractors can help themselves. Keep everything well marked.

- Paint

It is not advisable to put all the required paint on site at the same time, for a number of reasons. If a sub-contractor is involved, he will want to apply the top coat as soon as possible, so he can receive his final payment.

Painters also have a tendency to waist. On the larger contracts, deliver only what is necessary for a few days. If for example if there are a number of buildings or roofs on the same site that have to be painted, then calculate how much paint is needed for each section and allow only the correct amount on site for each area.

- Consumables

We only allow about 5% of the total material or paint costs to be allocated to this area. This can escalate very quickly of not controlled. For example, if you use a lot of sandpaper, then purchases it in large rolls and cut it into one square metre strips to be allocated to the site.

Keep small stock items of consumables that are used on a regular basis. Control accounts with hardware-stores that your staff have access to. This can be abused.

Use a system that does not allow for new paint brushes, rollers, scrapers and so on, to be given out every time they are asked for. The old items should be returned and inspected before new items are issued.

Notes:

14. **Notice to start painting** B10

It is polite to inform residents in a residential complex or tenants in an office environment, when you intend to start work on their unit or office. The following letter is an example of what you can send out.

Date 29th August

To all residents / tenants /owner
Unit number   / office number / shop number
Dear resident / tenant / owner

IMPORTANT NOTICE

PAINT PROJECT: YOUR UNIT / OFFICE / SHOP

1. The contractor intends to perform work with regard to the execution of the contract, to your property between 29th August and 9th December
2. In the circumstances you are requested to ensure that the contractor will be able to gain access to your property on the said date (s) by leaving the garden gates / office doors open or to make suitable arrangements for the unlocking thereof.
3. Please ensure that all windows are kept closed during preparation time and open during painting time and that all ornamental items that can be removed from external walls are taken down until the entire contract has been completed.
4. Please advise about pets, creepers to walls and any other special requirements.
5. Please note that we do not include the painting of front and back doors or security gates. If you require these to be done at an extra charge, please contact us for special arrangements.

Your co-operation is appreciated,
Kind regards,

THE CONTRACTOR

15. **Notice when painting is completed** B11

Snag lists, or items that have not been completed to both your staff's or the clients satisfaction, can be easily controlled with the following letter. It also circumvents the possible non payment from the client, stating that the contract has not been completed. If the letter is not returned by a prescribed date, you will assume the client is happy with the painting.

Date 29th August
To all residents / tenants / owner
Unit number   / office number / shop number
Dear resident / tenant / owner

IMPORTANT NOTICE

PAINT PROJECT: YOUR UNIT /OFFICE / SHOP

Please note that by the ___________, the contractor will be complete with the painting of your unit / office. We require that you assist us by inspecting your office / unit and listing any queries or complaints so we may address them for you.

These should be returned to unit / office number ________ by _________. Please also inspect all common areas to the buildings.

____

____

____

Should we not receive this letter back from you, we will assume you are happy with our work.

Many thanks

The Contractor

16. Using paint

Using old paint
- Once a paint tin is opened, oxygen changes the chemical structure
- Filter the paint, using fine gauze
- If you are using it to touch up an existing painted area, try a small section in a corner. The old paint may have faded and the colours will not match.
- If you have more than one tin of the same colour, mix them together to avoid discrepancies in colour.

Thinning paint.
- Not all paint can be thinned. Check the tin for technical information.
- When spray painting, it is often necessary to thin the paint.
- Water based paints are seldom thinned down.
- Oil based paints do not usually require thinning down at all.

Notes:

PART 11 – EQUIPMENT AND TOOLS

1. Spray guns

The typical spray machine used in the paint contracting industry is called an airless gun. It works off a diaphragm and sucks the paint directly from the drum, into the nozzle, which can be regulated.

Spray guns can speed up a contract by up to 10 times. If one man can roll or brush about 100 square metres per day, a spray gun team of two people can spray up to 1000 square metres per day.

Spraying can be done effectively on roofs, inside and outside on new buildings, boundary walls, floors and the external areas of buildings that need refurbishing.

It is recommended that you ask your spray gun supplier to visit a site where you can spray and give training to the operators. Huge savings can be made if you use a WFT (wet film thickness gauge) to monitor the thickness of paint you are applying.

If you need a final coat of 25 microns and you are spraying with the nozzle a little close and finish with 50 microns, you will use exactly double the amount of paint. This can easily happen.

In countries with higher labour costs, spraying is used far more often than emerging markets. All sorts of add-ons such as masking equipment is available to make the spraying easier and faster. There are invaluable tips on the internet for spraying applications.

2. Hydro-blasters

High pressure cleaning is such an important tool in your business. Not only can they speed up preparation time, but they can add a new product or service to your business and increase revenue. High pressure cleaning moldy or old roofs, cleaning of driveways, or washing dusty face bricks can add value to your business.

There are essentially two types of hydro-blasters: electric and petrol driven. Both types come in different makes, models and sizes. Do not buy cheap versions from your local discount store – the machine simply will not cope, being used eight hours every day. Rather go directly to your chosen supplier who will in turn give better prices and faster turn around time with maintenance and support.

The petrol driven machines are heavier, but useful if you have to wash in remote areas where electricity is difficult to access. You can of course use a generator if you only have electric models.

Essentially hydro-blasters can be adjusted to your needs. A closer nozzle to the surface or a thinner more directed jet of water will take off more old paint, dirt and grime than if the nozzle is set on wide and is further away from the surface.

These machines can be very dangerous, so precautions must be taken and the operator properly trained.

3. **Scaffolding**
    Up until two stories high, you have the choice of using either scaffolding or long step ladders. The problem with scaffolding is that you often have to break it down to move it (unless of course you have wheels and a flat surface to move it) or get many labourers to assist in the moving.

    Ladders on the other hand are easy to move and more versatile.

    Safety regulations change between regions, but basic safety rules have to be followed.

    Above two stories, you normally have to make use of a qualified scaffolding erector (even if moving the scaffolding on site). This is easy if you are using a hiring company and the prices are included with the initial erection, but expensive to keep asking the rental company to send someone to assist with the moving every day.

The best solution is firstly to slowly invest in good quality scaffolding of your own and get a few of your workers qualified in erecting scaffolding. You will save a small fortune down the road.

Aluminium scaffolding is the lightest and does not rust. It is however more expensive. If you purchase steel scaffolding, keep it rust free and painted.

4. Step ladders

There are a variety of ladder styles to choose from - some multipurpose ladders can handle many jobs, but some jobs require specific ladder designs to be done safely.

There are basic step and extension ladders, as well as platform, twin step, telescoping multi-ladder, multi-purpose ladders, and tripods. Step ladders are what most of us think of when we hear the word ladder - rungs set between two side rails, usually in an A-frame form.

Step ladders can be up to 4 metres tall. Extension ladders are made up of sliding sections that can be slid out and extended to reach up to 7 metres or more. Most extension ladders are designed to rest against the work surface. Once you determine a style of ladder, the next choice is what the ladder is made of.

Wooden ladders are mostly a thing of the past, as most ladders are now made of fiberglass or aluminum. Aluminum is more dangerous when working around electrical wires, but its light weight makes it attractive.

Keep your ladders well marked with their own unique number and keep an annual inspection record of the condition of each ladder. Do not hesitate to destroy ladders that are unsafe.

5. Moisture metre

Moisture metres are used for measuring the moisture content in concrete, plastered surfaces or wood. There are so many different types, but a general purpose machine should assist with all applications.

It has pins to determine the surface moisture, but can be used with insulated deep water probes or a hammer electrode. These hand held metres have digital displays and are simple to use. Their read-out is a given as a percentage of moisture on the surface, which only gives an indication of the moisture.

Moisture can only travel upwards to a maximum of 1,2 metres and stops. This is because of gravity. Any reading above this level will indicate either moisture from behind the wall (a high level of soil) or a plumbing problem in the wall itself.

If paint is applied over a damp area, it is highly likely that the damp will win and the paint will flake or become wet and dark. Using a moisture metre effectively, will add the option of damp proofing to your services.

Some paint contractors elect not to undertake damp proofing, but rather sub-contract it out or put the onus on the client to sort it out.

Either way, if you offer painting, you have to sort the damp problem out or pass the problem back to the client.

6. **Paint brushes and rollers**

Spray painting may be fast, but fine painting deserves the attention that only a brush can give. The slight imperfections left by each pass of the bristles give the job a warmer, richer feel.

Brushes are a necessity on most paint jobs for their ability to reach tight corners and cut in along trim. Moistened by a dip in fresh paint, good bristles line up to form a sharp tip that traces around sash and sill, defines the edge of the wall and ceiling, and lays paint over a windowsill without spattering the glass.

Only a quality brush can pull off such feats. So return the favor by cleaning and combing it out after every use.

Acrylic paints, which account for more than 90 percent of sales, go on best with a synthetic brush of nylon and polyester filaments

Natural-bristle brushes have traditionally been used to apply oil paints, polyurethanes, and varnishes, although a new class of oil-friendly synthetics is now challenging bristles' dominance in this realm.

General advice on paint brushes and rollers
Brushes – keep clean and use new ones if the bristles are worn out
- 25mm straight brush for windows, skirting's
- 75mm straight brush for door frames and trim work
- 100mm straight brush for ceilings and wall surrounds
- Angled brush for cutting in
- Hang with wire when drying, do not dry on the bristles
- Use a round handle for cutting in and trim work
- Use a flat handle for bigger areas
- The length should be 50% longer than the width

Rollers
- Lambs wool for acrylic
- Mohair for enamel
- Plastic for texture or ripple
- Dry hanging up

The correct way of dipping a paint brush into paint

- Dip the brush directly into the paint up to 1/3 of the length of the bristles. This stops the brush from being overloaded with paint and prevents dripping.
- Tap both sides of the brush lightly against the side of the can or pail. This loads the paint more on the interior of the brush.
- Do not scrape the paint off the brush by dragging across the edge of the bucket. That just removes the paint and makes the brush ineffective

7. Stirrers and mixing paint

Should paint be stirred or mixed? The answer is most definitely yes. Some paints need more stirring than others and if paint has been left for a period of time, then even more mixing is required.

You can use a hand held mixer or an attachment for your drilling machine. Paint shops have a vibrating mixer or shaker to make sure the job is properly done. Hand held mixers should preferably be a flat paddle, rather than a round pole or stick. This makes the mixing process easier.

Paint shops and hardware stores have a range of drill attachments. It will depend if you are out on site and often without the luxury of electricity or equipment.

8. Drop sheets or drop cloths

So much money can be saved if drop sheets are used in the painting process. This can be inside or even outside.

The cost of removing old unwanted spilt paint can mount up and annoy your client. If it is enamel paint, it may be impossible to remove without scratching the surface.

All paint shops sell drop sheets of some description. Make sure you replace them if they become too messy, which will make your contract look untidy and unprofessional.

Inside soft cotton sheeting is great, because of potential damage to furniture. Outside cheap plastic sheeting is easier, because of potential water damage. Simple newspaper is better than nothing.

9. Masking

There is an entire business, just in the masking of areas that are not to be painted. Masking done correctly, can save you a fortune. It is crucial to train your staff well and keep reminding them of the importance of correct masking procedures.

- Clear out the Workspace

It's always better to remove an item than to mask it. For interior jobs, light fixtures, switch plates and outlet covers should be removed. To avoid losing the screws, either replace them in their holes or use masking tape to affix them to the items they go with.

Outside, unhook hoses, remove planters, toys, and patio furniture, and consider parking your car on the street if it's near the work area.

- Cover Everything That's Left

Many items cannot be removed and must be covered. Some items you may need are:

Drop cloths - These are mainly used to protect the floor or sidewalk from drips.

- Tapes

Several varieties are available. Painter's tape, is the standard for attaching plastic or paper to almost any surface. This tape is available in several widths, from 1cm to 4cm. Its adhesive is strong and can be difficult to remove after a few hours, or when exposed to heat or sunlight. In some countries, painters tape can be difficult to come by, so alternative masking tapes should be used.

If your project involves lacquers or enamels, which can dissolve most adhesives, you'll want to use a high adhesive solvent tape. These tapes are specially developed to hold up to exposure to hot solvents.

Tape can be used by itself, to create straight edges and decorative effects, or it can be used to hold your masking paper or plastic film in place.

- Masking materials

It's important to use commercially available masking materials. Newspaper disintegrates when wet and can leave ink stains; regular plastic film is hard to handle and attach. A hand held masking machine dispenses specialized paper or plastic film, attaches the tape, and cuts it to the appropriate length. Again, these may not be readily available in all areas.

Masking paper is available in two varieties: regular brown kraft-style paper, which is cheap and easy to find, and a more expensive green variety for use with enamels, lacquers, and other high-solvent finishes.

Plastic masking film is heavier than most general purpose plastic films, and easier to handle. It is available in several widths, from 60cm to 250cm. Conveniently, the plastic is sized to fit popular window and door sizes.

- Exterior Paint Masking

Exterior paint masking includes windows, doors, trim, brick, deck floor, handrail, and sidewalks. Don't forget about fixtures like water valves, phone and communication boxes, electrical meters and lights.

Cover fences, plants, and shrubs with heavy drop cloths.

For wooden decks and other horizontal surfaces, place the drop cloths a few inches from the house and use a masking machine and masking paper to cover the edge close to the house. Attach the paper to the drop cloth with wide tape.

Outside, vertical walls can be masked the same way as interior surfaces. Just be aware that on rough surfaces, like brick, masonry, and concrete, the painter's tape often will not adhere well. Try to attach the tape to a painted surface instead.

Windows and doors should be completely covered for the best results when undertaking exterior painting projects.

Whether painting indoors or out, using high quality paint, brushes, and rollers can·help reduce splatters.

- Spray Painting

Tight seals and complete coverage are essential when spray painting. Overspray is impossible to control, especially outdoors, where it may be windy.

- Windows, Doors, and Cabinets

Completely covering windows, doors, and cabinetry is important if you will be spray painting. The plastic film is faster to apply than masking paper. Using the film dispenser, attach an appropriate length of plastic film to the top of the frame.

If you're painting the ceiling and don't want to change your wall color, or if you need to protect an accent wall, you can drape the entire wall in plastic. Use

4cm tape, attached horizontally to the wall. Leave the bottom half of the tape free; position the plastic underneath, then press firmly to adhere. Finish by sealing the side and bottom edges of the plastic.

Pull down the plastic and tack the bottom corners with two small pieces of tape. Next, tape the edges to the wall, creating a tight seal. Be careful not to leave any gaps.

- Ceilings

For smooth or textured ceilings (not acoustic) you can apply masking to protect from overspray if you're painting walls. Attach wide masking tape along the perimeter of the ceiling, then, using a dispenser, attach wide masking paper to the tape. You'll need to overlap the paper to ensure complete coverage.

Plastic can be attached the same way and provides better coverage than the paper does.

Take the time to properly protect your work area. Masking everything that can't be removed will save you hours of frustration and touch-ups!

Wooden decks and fences also require covering or you will be forced to clean then sand and refinish. Drop cloths are your first defense.

10. Painters tool kit

A basic painter's tool kit consists of the following:
Abrasive Pads
Broom
Brush
Bucket
Cloths
Dust Sheets / drop cloth
Dust Mask
Eye Protection, Goggles
Fan for ventilation
Filler and filler knife (thin and thick)

Fungicidal Wash
Gloves, chemical resistant
Knee pads
Ladder, step
Masking Tape, Painter's Tape
Paint Remover
Paper towels
Pliers
Primer, masonry,
Primer, wood
Putty
Putty Knife (stiff and flexible)
Respirator
Roller kit (including tray)
Rubbish Bags
Sand Paper, different grades
Scraper, shaped and straight
Screwdriver
Sealant, clear and white
Sealant Gun
Sponge
Wood filler

It's better to work smarter than harder.

11. Caulking gun

A caulking gun allows you to dispense a variety of semi-liquid products to seal gaps around sinks, toilets and other fixtures, as well as waterproofing and so on.

Different types of products that can be dispensed from a caulking gun include polyurethane, acrylics and sealers.

There are cheap hand pump type guns to battery operated guns. Choose good quality guns that will last years.

12. Power sanders

After scraping off loose paint, the use of power sanders is highly recommended. Often sanding previously painted surfaces can identify and remove additional loose and peeling paint. Plus the finished look will be much better when compared to scraping alone.

Power sanders can be used on new and old wood surfaces as well as sanding stained wood decks prior to refinishing.

13. Roller poles and extensions

An important piece of a paint rolling system is a roller pole. A good roller pole is positive locking and comfortable to use. Much better than using a threaded broom stick. Many styles are available in different lengths; definitely buy the best you can afford.

14. Power roller

Power Rollers are sold as stand alone units ready to be used as is or as an accessory that can be purchased and attached to an airless sprayer. The stand alone power rollers sold through paint stores or hardware stores are weak machines that are often more frustrating to use than helpful. The power roller accessories designed for professional use can be cumbersome but will apply a lot of paint faster and produce better results.

15. Paint scrapers

Choosing a good paint scraping tool will easily pay for itself. A paint scraping blade needs to perform many tasks quickly and comfortably. Removing loose paint, as well as other old materials, is a basic painting task. Plus scraping paint is an important first step in the preparation process.

16. Heat guns

These are used to blast the painted surface with blistering heat. As the paint blisters, you can scrape it off with a scraper or stripping tool. It can be very slow, so cost it in accordingly.

PART 12 – SAFETY

G   A comprehensive safety plan is on the disc, with the following templates:

- Corporate health & safety policy statement
- Health & safety specification
    Purpose
    Applicability
    Normative references
    Definitions
    Responsibilities
    Task & hazard identification
    Additional requirements
- Site establishment check list for contractors
- Appointment of the assistant construction supervisor
- Appointment of the batch plant supervisor
- Appointment of the site health & safety officer
- Appointment of the construction supervisor
- Appointment of the fall protection plan developer
- Appointment of the fire extinguisher inspector
- Appointment of the formwork and support work supervisor
- Appointment of the ladder supervisor
- Appointment of the material hoist inspector
- Appointment of the construction site risk assessor
- Appointment of the scaffolding risk assessor
- Appointment of the suspended platform supervisor
- Scaffolding assessment list
- Competent person scaffold inspection check list
- First aid box equipment check list
- Hand tools and equipment check list
- Hazardous substance check list
- Walking-walking surfaces
- Ladder inspection check list
- Personal protection check list
- Portable electrical tools register
- Public safety check list

- Roofing check list
- Appointment first aid officer
- Equipment register
- Stepladder inspection form
- Scaffolding inspection form
- Incident report form
- Safety work procedures – ladders
- Safety work procedures – heights
- Heath & safety responsibilities
- Health & safety representative
- Joint health & safety representative
- Safety support staff
- Workers
- Subcontractors
- Safety training
- General safety & equipment

General Safety

The main areas to protect are the skin and clothing, eyes and lungs and of course the prevention of accidents at heights.

- Protect exposed skin from caustic chemicals.
- Protect the eyes from paint chips or drips.
- Protect the lungs from dust or spray mist.

Skin and clothing protection can be as easy as wearing old cloths (recommended) or wearing disposable overalls. Disposable overalls will cover everything except the hands, feet and head.

1. Hard hats
   Hard hats are mandatory on all building sites as well as special safety zones. It may not be critical to wear hard hats on a normal painting site, but if it is necessary, do not hesitate to hand them out.
2. Safety harnesses

Safety harnesses have to be worn by law in most regions, on scaffolding and at heights (normally above 3 metres). There are many different types, but the safest are the ones with built-in flexibility, in case of a fall.

3. Safety shoes

    Also mandatory on all building sites. On a normal painting contract for example a single story house, it would not really be necessary.

4. Gloves

    Neoprene gloves are the best way to protect your hands from exposure to solvents or dangerous chemicals.

5. Goggles and eye protection

    Used to protect the eyes. Good quality hardened plastic goggles are the best. Protection can be against dust from sanding machines, spray painting, flaking and chipping paint and even mixing and drilling.

6. Ladders

    The ladders that are most dangerous are extension ladders and there are two primary pieces of safety equipment that you should own.

- *Ladder levelers* are an absolute must and very useful for both interior as well as exterior painting. The principal is very basic; attach a set of adjustable legs to the ladder to keep it level on varying terrain, much better than piling rocks or wood to stabilize the ladder and

- *The pot hook* is an incredibly basic accessory but one that your painters should not do without. This simple and very inexpensive accessory allows you to work and still have one hand firmly holding the ladder.
- Never stand on the top rung or on the roller tray shelf.
- Make sure your ladder stands firmly on all four legs.
- Avoid overreaching. Move your ladder frequently.

7. Scaffolding

    Scaffolding has its own set of safety rules and regulations and should be adhered to. Check with your local safety council and ask for a scaffolding check list.

8. Masks for inhalation and respirators - Dust masks and chemical respirators are an absolute must have, for painting tools in many situations. The primary dangers are from sanding, spraying and using aromatic solvents. Sanding presents a difficult challenge, especially when working on old finishes.

PART 13 – DEALING WITH LABOUR

1. Sub-contractors vs. hiring your own labour

If you receive a paint contract, you have two choices. You can hire labour to do the painting, or you can sub-contract to an independent painting team.

Hiring labour usually means it is based on a long term commitment. You will be paying monthly salaries and perks that you have negotiated. You will also pay tax and any other legal requirements that go with the contracting fraternity.

Sub-contractors on the other hand pay their own tax and no perks or government requirements will have to be paid.

So why hire labour? Sub-contractors do not have permanent work so they are usually more expensive. But, as soon as the contract is over, you do not pay their salaries, so your overheads decrease drastically.

Your own labour on the other hand, are usually more loyal, better trained and experienced and know your equipment more intimately.

It really is a trade-off between the two. You have to decide, but a middle path is to hire your own core of labour and sub-contract the rest of the work. This way you can grow the business quickly if you are inundated with work and shrink without overheads when you need to as well.

2. Finding and keeping the right people

When you start a new paint contracting business or need extra painters quickly for a new contract there are a few ways to employ painters.

- Advertise. You will be surprised how many responses you receive. An advertisement for sub-contractors could read like this:

"Painting sub-contractors required in the xyz area, with own transport and trade references. Phone 999-999-999"

- Ask your local paint store. Most paint stores have business cards or at least names of good painters or painting crews that are looking for work. These are usually experienced painters.
- The internet is a good way of finding larger sub-contractors, but also specialized crews such as painters who are qualified to work at heights or erect scaffolding.
- Newspapers often carry classified advertisements offering painting services or painters looking for jobs.

3. **Rewards and incentives**

   Financial bonuses on contracts are a good way to motivate labour, especially sub-contractors. The danger is that they want to complete the contract as fast as possible and will often take short cuts.

   Once the final coat of paint is on the walls, the contract will be deemed to be complete. But has the hydro-blasting been done properly? Or has the primer or even first coat of paint been applied?

   The up-side is that the contract will be finished in record time. Because everyone is on a bonus incentive, they tend to motivate each other. Self management comes into play. The only sure way to monitor the workmanship is through a quality control system, whereby each step is inspected and signed off by management.

   Bonuses can be given in a number of ways.
- Total for the contract. This is the easiest way. You just take a percentage of the contract and allocate it to labour. But how do they get paid? Who says they are now 50% complete? Remember there are many stages to painting including preparation, patch priming, priming, first coat and final coat.

   You have to work out the percentage together.
- A more complicated way, but more accurate way is to break the contract down into the different stages of painting and allocate a percentage to each stage. For example a contract may be $1,000 and the labour portion about 25%, or $250. Or the rate to paint is $20 per square metre and there are 50 square metres to paint. Of the $20, the labour portion is 25%, or $5 per sqm.

No	Description	%
1	Hydro-washing	20%
2	Prepare cracks	20%
3	Priming	20%
4	First coat	20%
5	Final coat	20%

So once the preparation is complete (i.e. hydro-washing and crack filling) you can pay 40% of either the total labour allowed (40% of $250 = $100) or 40% of the labour rate allowed. (40% of $5 x 50sqm = $100)

Either way, the results are the same.

4. **Contracts** F1

   There are different types of contracts, for example, for employing a sales representative (which could be changed to suite any employed person) and a sub-contractors agreement.

5. **Sub contractors fees**

   You normally agree up front with your sub contractor what the fees will be on the contract. These need to be monitored on a daily basis.

PART 14 – FINANCE

1. The difference between financial accounting and financial management

To run your business professionally and profitably, you have to manage your finance according to accepted business practices. This means you will have to spend some of your profits on recording your financial transactions.

There are two types of financial controls. Financial accounting and financial management.

Financial accounting is the function of bookkeeping and is important for the following reasons:
- It is a legal requirement for taxes and company reporting.
- It shows important information such as profit or loss, ratios which reflect percentages and relationships between different financial indicators.
- The main two reports are the balance sheet and the income statement, which summarises the activities of the business. The balance sheet reports on the Assets and Liabilities of a company.
- The income statement shows the sales revenue and expenses. These expenses are split into the costs incurred while running a site, which are variable and the costs incurred on a monthly basis, which we call overheads.
- To work out what the business is worth if you want to sell it one day.

Financial management on the other hand is the movement of funds, usually starting with a budget of what you might expect to turn over and then comparing it to actual expenses.

A cash flow projection will be used to monitor the cash flow and steer the company.

Normally we will employ a book keeper to do the financial accounting, full or part time. Then a suitably qualified accountant will scrutinize the books and sign them off for legal and management decision making.

In summary, you should always have your finger on the pulse and run your own financial management and you should outsource the function of financial accounting or book keeping.

2. Ratio analysis

What is ratio analysis? The Balance Sheet and the Income Statement are essential, but they are only the starting point for successful financial management. Apply Ratio Analysis to Financial Statements to analyze the success, failure, and progress of your business.

Ratio Analysis enables the business owner/manager to spot trends in a business and to compare its performance and condition with the average performance of similar businesses in the same industry. To do this compare your ratios with the average of businesses similar to yours and compare your own ratios for several successive years, watching especially for any unfavorable trends that may be starting. Ratio analysis may provide the all-important early warning indications that allow you to solve your business problems before your business is destroyed by them.

Balance Sheet Ratio Analysis Formula

Important Balance Sheet Ratios measure liquidity and solvency (a business's ability to pay its bills as they come due) and leverage (the extent to which the business is dependent on creditors' funding). They include the following ratios:

Liquidity Ratios

These ratios indicate the ease of turning assets into cash. They include the Current Ratio, Quick Ratio, and Working Capital.

Current Ratios. The Current Ratio is one of the best known measures of financial strength. It is figured as shown below:

$$\text{Current Ratio} = \frac{\text{Total Current Assets}}{\text{Total Current Liabilities}}$$

The main question this ratio addresses is: "Does your business have enough current assets to meet the payment schedule of its current debts with a margin of safety for possible losses in current assets, such as inventory shrinkage or collectable accounts?" A generally acceptable current ratio is 2 to 1. But whether or not a specific ratio is satisfactory depends on the nature of the business and the characteristics of its current assets and liabilities. The minimum acceptable current ratio is obviously 1:1, but that relationship is usually playing it too close for comfort.

If you decide your business's current ratio is too low, you may be able to raise it by:

- Paying some debts or creditors
- Increasing your current assets from loans or other borrowings with a maturity of more than one year.
- Converting non-current assets into current assets.
- Increasing your current assets from new equity contributions.
- Putting profits back into the business.

Quick Ratios. The Quick Ratio is sometimes called the "acid-test" ratio and is one of the best measures of liquidity. It is figured as shown below:

$$\text{Quick Ratio} = \frac{\text{Cash+debtors}}{\text{Total Current Liabilies}}$$

The Quick Ratio is a much more exacting measure than the Current Ratio. By excluding inventories or stock, it concentrates on the really liquid assets, with value that is fairly certain. It helps answer the question: "If all sales revenues should disappear, could my business meet its current obligations with the readily convertible `quick' funds on hand?"

An acid-test of 1:1 is considered satisfactory unless the majority of your "quick assets" are in debtors and the pattern of debtors collection lags behind the schedule for paying current liabilities. (try and keep collection to 7 days)

Working Capital. Working Capital is more a measure of cash flow than a ratio. The result of this calculation must be a positive number. It is calculated as shown below:

Working Capital = Total Current Assets - Total Current Liabilities

Bankers look at Net Working Capital over time to determine a company's ability to weather financial crisis. Loans are often tied to minimum working capital requirements.

A general observation about these three Liquidity Ratios is that the higher they are the better, especially if you are relying to any significant extent on creditor money to finance assets.

Leverage Ratio

This Debt/Worth or Leverage Ratio indicates the extent to which the business is reliant on debt financing (creditor money versus owner's equity):

$$\text{Debt/Worth Ratio} = \frac{\text{Total Liabilities}}{\text{Net Worth}}$$

Generally, the higher this ratio, the more risky a creditor will perceive its exposure in your business, making it correspondingly harder to obtain credit.

Income Statement Ratio Analysis

The following important State of Income Ratios measure profitability:

Gross Margin Ratio

This ratio is the percentage of sales dollars left after subtracting the cost of goods sold from net sales. It measures the percentage of sales dollars remaining (after obtaining or manufacturing the goods sold) available to pay the overhead expenses of the company.

Comparison of your business ratios to those of similar businesses will reveal the relative strengths or weaknesses in your business. The Gross Margin Ratio is calculated as follows:

$$\text{Gross Margin Ratio} = \frac{\text{Gross Profit}}{\text{Net Sales}}$$

(Gross Profit = Net Sales - Cost of Goods Sold)

Net Profit Margin Ratio

This ratio is the percentage of sales dollars left after subtracting the Cost of Goods sold and all expenses, except income taxes. It provides a good opportunity to compare your company's "return on sales" with the performance of other companies in your industry. It is calculated before income tax because tax rates and tax liabilities vary from company to company for a wide variety of reasons, making comparisons after taxes much more difficult. The Net Profit Margin Ratio is calculated as follows:

$$\text{Net Profit Margin Ratio} = \frac{\text{Net Profit Before Tax}}{\text{Net Sales}}$$

Management Ratios

Other important ratios, often referred to as Management Ratios, are also derived from Balance Sheet and Statement of Income information.

Stock or Inventory Turnover Ratio (Paint contractors usually have no stock)

This ratio reveals how well inventory is being managed. It is important because the more times inventory can be turned in a given operating cycle, the greater the profit. The Stock Turnover Ratio is calculated as follows:

$$\text{Stock Turnover Ratio} = \frac{\text{Net Sales}}{\text{Average Inventory at Cost}}$$

Debtors Turnover Ratio

This ratio indicates how well debtors are being collected. If debtors are not collected reasonably in accordance with their terms, management should rethink its collection policy. If debtors are excessively slow in being converted to cash, liquidity could be severely impaired. The Debtors Turnover Ratio is calculated as follows:

$$\text{Daily Credit Sales} = \frac{\text{Net Credit Sales/Year}}{\text{365 Days/Year}}$$

$$\text{Debtors Turnover (in days)} = \frac{\text{Debtors}}{\text{Daily Credit Sales}}$$

Return on Assets Ratio

This measures how efficiently profits are being generated from the assets employed in the business when compared with the ratios of firms in a similar business. A low ratio in comparison with industry averages indicates an inefficient use of business assets. The Return on Assets Ratio is calculated as follows:

$$\text{Return on Assets} = \frac{\text{Net Profit before Tax}}{\text{Total Assets}}$$

Return on Investment (ROI) Ratio.

The ROI is perhaps the most important ratio of all. It is the percentage of return on funds invested in the business by its owners. In short, this ratio tells the owner whether or not all the effort put into the business has been worthwhile. If the ROI is less than the rate of return on an alternative, risk-free investment such as a bank savings account, the owner may be wiser to sell the company, put the money in such a savings instrument, and avoid the daily struggles of small business management. The ROI is calculated as follows:

$$\text{Return on Investment} = \frac{\text{Net Profit before Tax}}{\text{Net Worth}}$$

These ratios allow you to identify trends in your business and to compare its progress with the performance of others. You may therefore determine your business's relative strengths and weaknesses.

3. Cash flow

Cash flow is the life blood of all businesses. Use the basic rules of cash flow, to build the paint contracting business you have always dreamed about.

Understanding your cash flow, means you have to understand how it works. Basically you need to know the following:

- How much cash is in the bank now?
- How much cash will be in the bank in the future?
- What expenses that need to be paid now must I deduct?
- What expenses in the future will need to be paid, do I need to deduct?
- What income is coming in now and in the future?
- Cash is hard cash, cash in the bank and in the future, it can even be debtors (money owing to you)

The items above define all the variables in a cash flow. The cash flow rules are as follows:

- Never run out of cash
- Know you cash balance now
- Do your cash flow today or get someone else to do it for you
- Don't confuse your bank balance and your cash flow
- Know your cash flow six months in advance
- Cash flow problems do not just happen
- Have cash flow projections
- Take care of collecting money

4. **Projections** E1

There are a few important items to remember when projecting your cash flow into the future.

- You have two different types of expenses that come off your account. Monthly overheads which could be insurances, salaries, car expenses and so on. These could be money that you have to pay out by EFT or check, or even debit orders.

Either way, you have to project into the future when these amounts have to be accounted for in your projections.

- Then the income is a projection of your bank balance now, debtors that owe you money to and work in progress that still needs to be invoiced, but has not been completed yet.

Creditors or money that you owe, is easy to calculate once product has been ordered.. You normally have 30 days from statement to pay.

But, calculating future expenses that will need to be paid from work in progress (or orders in hand that have not been completed yet) is far more difficult.

You will make mistakes in the beginning, but get closer to the mark as you get more experienced. This is why budgeting a contract and then recording the exact profits, it so crucial.

You have to estimate both the materials and labour you will be using in the future.

The disc has an Excel spreadsheet that does your cash flow projection for you. E1

5. Example of a balance sheet and income statement

The income statement only shows a portion of a businesses' financial picture. Perhaps there are excellent profits being made, but what about its debt load? (i.e. is the business holding too debt much in relation to its profit?) As well, the other financial statements don't give a good enough view to a bank manager or loan company just how solvent a company is (meaning: what ability the business has to liquidate its assets to potentially pay off its debts). A strong balance sheet equates to a better lending risk.

Income statement is income less expenses, equals profit less taxes, equals net profit.

Sample income statement for the paint contracting industry:

Total revenue		**100%**
Cost of paint	20%	
Cost of consumables	5%	
Cost of labour	25%	**50%**
Gross profit		**50%**
Operating expenses		**10%**
Commissions for sales		**5%**
Operating profit		**35%**
Tax (30% of OP)		**10%**
Profit after tax		**25%**

A balance sheet is liabilities plus equity equals assets

ASSETS

- current assets + cash in the bank + petty cash = net cash (by totaling the previous three items);
- stock + debtors + net cash = total current assets
- fixed assets + land + buildings - depreciation = net land and buildings
- equipment - depreciation = net equipment
- total assets

LIABILITIES

- creditors + wages payable + taxes payable = total current liabilities
- long term loans + bond = total long term liabilities
- total liabilities

EQUITY

- owners equity + owners earnings + retained earnings + current earnings = total earnings
- total equity

6. **Invoice samples**   E2

   An invoice should have all the necessary information for you and your client to cross reference. If is not the final invoice, then it should say so.

   An invoice reference number should be generated (often this is done by a computerised program), which could show your company's initials plus the date. Or the number of invoices generated for that month followed by the date:

   PCI03/09/2011 where PCI is **P**aint **C**ontractor **I**nvoice(your company initials) followed by 03 (3rd invoice for that month) and the date.

7. Factoring

Factoring is an alternative to a bank overdraft. It offers working capital for your business based on releasing vital cash flow which is tied up in unpaid invoices and outstanding debtors.

For many smaller and growing businesses, the debtor's book is the most valuable asset. If your customers are other businesses, factoring can often provide your business with the capital it needs based on your debtors-book.

Factoring is a method of releasing the money tied up in book debts, thus substantially replacing credit sales with cash sales. The facility includes professional debtor administration, as well as collection and credit management.

Consider factoring as a way to finance your sales. If your sales go up, the amount of your financing automatically goes up. Cash flow crunches can be avoided and you don't have to worry about slow-paying customers.

8. Management accounts on a regular basis

Remember, it does not matter just how good you are at paint contracting, if your cash slips away from you, you will fail.

If your business is just starting or is still small, consider the following guide to managing your accounts regularly.

- Outsource the accounting function to someone who possibly works from home. They can come in once a week and record all the transactions.
- If your business has grown, then purchase one of the many efficient software programs for accounting and either record the transactions yourself or hire someone within your company to do it for you.
- Do your own cash flow projections on a daily basis
- Keep records for five years
- Analyze your financial situation on a regular basis and learn from your mistakes or triumphs.

9. Keep debtors days to 7

This means you want to keep your debtors (money owning to you) within 7 days of invoicing. So if you have an interim invoice during the contract, try and collect it within 7 days.

If your paint purchases are on 30 days from statement and you pay your labour for example every 2 weeks, you only need cash flow for labour (about 25% of the contract value). If you collect your money faster than you need to spend it, your entire business will flourish and you should not have cash flow problems.

10. Petty cash

Cash has a way of getting away from you. It is normally used for those emergency items on site on a daily basis. Try and have small consumables on hand in stock and record them as an expense onto each and every site.

If you have a large site for a long period of time, consider opening up a hardware account at a hardware where you have negotiated prices, terms and who signs on the account. (But monitor the purchases carefully).

Petty cash should be accounted for every day and the expenses allocated to the different sites.

11. Break even analysis

Breakeven analysis helps you calculate how much you need to sell before you begin to make a profit.

If your monthly fixed overheads are $10000 and your average gross profit margin is 50%, what is your break even point?

```
Sales                   20000
Gross profit (50%)10000
Overheads         10000
Net profit                  0
```

Therefore breakeven on 10000 overheads is 20000 at a gross profit margin of 50%.

The above is a simple example, but illustrates how easy it is to project sales in order to break even.

Notes:

PART 15 – CORPORATE GOVERNANCE 

1. Legal entities

Depending on your area, you have two main options in order to trade.

- *Sole trader.* This means that you will trade under your own name as ABC Paint contractor. Your bank account and taxes are the same as your company's.

  The problems with this system are that you will be personably liable if the company defaults on payments and clients like to see a professional image behind the company they are giving orders to.

- *Company.* Again, depending on the region you are in, there are a few options. Ask advice from your appointed accountant and choose a company legal vehicle that is low on taxes and accountant charges. You will however be more protected (but not if you have signed personal surety).

  Clients and even suppliers will see a company that is serious about being in business.

2. Bank accounts

Once you have set your company up, the first thing to do is set up your bank account. Also open a linked savings account that is higher on interest. If you are running your company properly and receiving regular payments, you should have excess money on hand most of the time.

Deal with your personal bankers who have a history with your banking details. It just makes life easier.

3. Tax

Never get behind on tax. Allow company tax, personal tax and VAT to be paid as an expense in your cash flow when necessary. The receiver of revenue is not someone you want to owe money to, since they charge very high rates of interest. Besides it is a criminal offence not to pay taxes.

4. Municipal bye laws

When you are ready to set your company up, check with your accountant what the bye laws are. They will include things like; you can not work from home. Or you can work from home but with only two employees.

Other laws include the way you get rid of paint and solvents as well as what signage you can erect for marketing on site as well as for advertising purposes.

5. Labour regulations

There are many labour regulations that may affect you. Local and national government have different rules as to what you have to pay for each employee on a regular basis.

The different payments are to cover health or unemployment. Check with your accountant.

Typical registrations you will have to attend to are:

- UIF –Unemployment insurance fund
- WCA –Workman's compensation association
- PAYE – Employees tax
- And any other government requirements in your area, specific to the services you offer.

Notes:

PART 16 – PLANNING FOR GROWTH

1. **Expansion has to have a new business plan**

   You original business plan has probably now been achieved and you are ready for the growth phase in your business.

   Now you need a different sort of plan, were everybody in your company subscribes to your new vision of growth.

   The following guidelines will help you with your growth plan:

   - Check that you are delivering your promises to your clients and if not start by fulfilling them.
   - Research your markets again, since you may find that your original markets have changed.
   - Rekindle a strong sense of purpose and share your vision with all your stakeholders, including clients, staff and suppliers.
   - Fine tune your marketing message to your clients. Why are they not placing more orders?
   - Check your resources and make sure you are ready to expand.
   - Close the sales and collect the cash. You may have many quotations out there waiting for orders, so look into this potential money pot and convert quotations into cash.
   - Check your own commitment and see that you are not the problem.

2. **Increasing profits not volumes**

   Do not make the fundamental mistake of taking on non profitable orders, but things look good on the outside because you have increased turnover.

   It is so easy to fill in tender after tender (so you think your activity is up) and put in prices that will ultimately give lower profits.

   Paint contractors often do this, not because they want to grow the business, but either because their cash flow looks bad in the future, so they think turnover will bail them out, or because they have excess labour they do not want to lose and they get new orders to keep the labourers busy.

3. **Learn to say no – Don't overtrade**
    You have to have a bench mark of what your expected profits should be. For example if you agree that your gross profit margins do not go below 40%, then stick to that principal
    It may be they go down to 30%, but possibly because you tendered incorrectly, rain delays caused profit loss or paint prices went up since you tendered.

    Overtrading can seriously affect your resources. If you only have 5 stepladders and need 10 because you have suddenly received new orders, you have two choices. Hire them at additional costs or purchase new ones. Either way you have to find excess cash.

    Notes:

PART 17 – PAINT CONTRACTING SECRETS

1. Cherry pickers

Working at heights can be so much easier if mobile platforms or cherry pickers are used. They are usually hired out on a daily or weekly basis and come in many different sizes.

Some are motorized and others towed. Either way, they are on wheels so a smooth surface is normally the only way they can get around. The price is off-set by the ease of getting to heights quickly.

Many contractors use so many cherry pickers, that the hire cost often outweighs their labour cost. But because of the speed, they actually make more profits. It is expensive to keep breaking scaffolding down and re-erecting it. Also, space may be a problem, or arched bridges are easy because you can keep adjusting the height or individual light fittings may need painting.

Cherry pickers used correctly can be one of paint contracting biggest secrets.

2. Subcontract labour

To hire your own, or sub-contract out. That is the question. In the chapter dealing with labour, this topic has been covered thoroughly, but you can not underestimate the savings, both in terms of money and hassles. sub-contracting out your labour can assist you.

3. Damp vs. waterproofing

Waterproofing is for roofs and damp proofing is for walls. If you do painting, you should offer damp proofing as well, if you want to avoid problems later with damp or peeling paint.

Waterproofing is a very specialised field and has nothing really to do with painting. Rather pass the leads on to a waterproofing company you know well.

4. Masking equipment & spray painting

The speed which you can do spray painting can be 10 to 5 times faster and save you a fortune in labour as well as paint, where the correct thickness has been applied.

Do your research and get the correct masking equipment to cover the areas you do not want painted.

Notes:

PART 18 – A FINAL WORD 

Paint contracting is a sophisticated business and run properly can make you wealthy. Some people treat painters as blue collar workers, but from experience I know that you can make much more than the local lawyer or accountant.

Put sound business principals into practice and develop a discipline for constant monitoring and recording. Knowing your past can assist with your future. Planning with a sound vision is already a winning formula.

Write your business plan down and visit it regularly. Follow trends and stay close to your labour, clients and suppliers.

Take orders only from clients who you know will pay and quote with a gross profit margin of at least 35% at the minimum. (50% is better)

Keep good records and put everything in writing to all stakeholders. This is just sound business practice.

To remain professional, learn everything there is to know about your business. Go on courses if offered from suppliers and read as much as you can on the internet. Become an expert.

Do a quality job – one you would do for yourself. You will stay in business much longer that way. Go the extra mile. Clients notice and referrals are the most powerful form of marketing.

Email me at info@franchisekit.co.za or visit www.franchisekit.co.za and I will endeavor to answer any your questions and offer advice where I can.

Kevin McGeer

Log onto
www.franchisekit.co.za
to download the
CD-ROM Templates
PAINT
contractor's
business manual